P9-BXZ-070

Teddy Bears
& STEIFF ANIMALS
SECOND SERIES

Margaret Fox Mandel

COLLECTOR BOOKS
A Division of Schroeder Publishing Co., Inc.

Acknowledgments

Acknowledgment is gratefully extended to the following who have graciously shared their toys and photographs. All photographs are by the author unless noted otherwise in parentheses.

Carolyn Altfather (herself); Kay Bransky (Art Bransky); Joanna Brunken (Carmin McWilliams); Mary Alice Carey; Jessie "Ted" Casciano (herself); Nancy Catlin (herself); Sammie Chambliss (herself); Sydney R. Charles (Maria Schmidt); Nancy Crane (Beverly Rudd); Linda Cron; Gwen Daniel (herself); Gaye N. Delling (David Delling); Betty DiBattista (Jessie "Ted" Casciano); Carolyn Dockray; The Enchanted Doll House; John R. Fazendin (himself); Dot Franklin (herself); Karen Frasco; Diane Gard (herself); Bill Gardner; Marianne Gardner; Betsy Gottschalk; Connie Hart; Gebr. Hermann KG; Dee Hockenberry (Tom Hockenberry and Candace Fasano); Diane Hoffman, Turn of the Century Antiques; Brenda Hoyle; Christine Irr (herself); Marlene Irwin; Pamela Johnson; Virginia Joy (herself); Beverly Krein; Barbara Lauver (Gary Funck); Linda K. Lilley (herself); Wanda Loukides (herself); Robin Lowe (herself); McArdle Family (Carolyn Altfather); Ellyn McCorkell; Carl McQueary; Chris McWilliams (Carmin McWilliams); David McWilliams (Carmin McWilliams); Stephanie Manley; Nan C. Moorehead (Art Owen); Rosemary Moran, My Favorite Dolls; Edward Moriuchi; J. Corey O'Brien (Maria Schmidt); Lisa Osta (herself); Beverly Port (herself); Margaret Rea (herself); Reeves Internatinal, Inc.; Kim Rehor; Colleen Ripley; Carol Rockwell; Nancy and Susan Roeder; Beth Savino, Hobby Center Toys (Ben Savino); Mary Schinhofen (herself); Maria Schmidt (herself); Claudia Shotwell (herself); Helen Sieverling (Glenn Sieverling); Jennifer Sisty (herself); Patricia R. Smith; Alice-Jane Sokol (N. Paul Holmgren); Lisa Stanziale; Margarete Steiff GmbH; Kirk Stines (himself); Tom and Susie Stroud; Kathy Teske; Kelly Tidwell (L.C. Tims, Jr.); Misty Tidwell (L.C. Tims, Jr.); Marge Vance; Jane L. Viprino (Rick Viprino); Roberta Viscusi (Gina Viscusi); Karen Watson; Marlene Wendt (herself); Peggy Young (herself).

The current values in this book should be used only as a guide. They are not intended to set prices, which vary from one section of the country to another. Auction prices as well as dealer prices vary greatly and are affected by condition as well as demand. Neither the Author nor the Publisher assumes responsibility for any losses that might be incurred as a result of consulting this guide.

Additional copies of this book may be ordered from:

Collector Books
P.o. Box 3009
Paducah, KY 42001

@$19.95. Add $1.00 for postage and handling.

Copyright: Margaret Fox Mandel, ·1987

This book or any part thereof may not be reproduced without the written consent of the Author and Publisher.

Table of Contents

I. Introduction

Theodore Roosevelt and the Teddy Bear

The best loved toy of all time was named after Theodore Roosevelt (President of the United States, 1901-1909).

Roosevelt was a leading field naturalist of his time, a hunter, rancher, explorer, soldier, prolific writer on diverse subjects, a devout conservationist who did more to preserve the American landscape than any American leader before or since, and of course, politician and President. He was the first American to win the Nobel Peace Prize (for helping end the Russo-Japanese War); he busted trusts and built the Panama Canal.

Though Roosevelt recognized the magic of the real bear in its natural environment and its appeal to the

Teddy Roosevelt and Friend, made in England by the House of Nisbet to commemorate the 125th anniversary of the President's birth, October 27, 1858. Produced in 1983 only: 7½"/19 cm., fine vinyl figure wearing a felt suit with leather belt, molded plastic hat, removable glasses; holding 1¾"/4.5 cm. unjointed vinyl Teddy Bear. The issue price of the boxed and tagged set was $70.00.

public mind, he seems never to have spoken publicly about the Teddy Bear. He never considered the animal a personal symbol and preferred the much less popular bull moose.* Nevertheless, on a hunting trip in November 1902, President Teddy Roosevelt refused to shoot an old sick bear that had been tied to a tree by other hunters. The issue was immortalized by Clifford Berryman, a political cartoonst for the *Washington Post*, who used the incident to illustrate a boundary dispute, depicting the animal as a shivering little bear cub. The worst hunt of Roosevelt's life forever linked his name to the bear. (See Illustration 1.).

In 1903, Margarete Steiff (in Germany) and Morris Michtom (in America, where he later founded the Ideal Novelty Company) crafted and sold toy bears. Soon they were called "Teddy Bears" and their commercial success was ensured.

Conservation and Restoration of Teddy Bears

The object of conservation is to protect from physical deterioration. Restoration refers to the putting back into nearly the original form. (See Illustrations 2 and 3).

The survival of an early straw stuffed Teddy Bear is endangered because of the high acid content of straw. Furthermore, its textile covering becomes dry with aging and tears with the slightest pressure. Dust is acidic and abrasive and will wear its fur down.

To reduce these dangers, gently vacuum the bear through a net. Do not display in sunlight or fluorescent light; use incandescent (tungsten) light bulbs which have no damaging ultraviolet rays. Exercise care in storage. Avoid high fluctuations in temperature. Be correct in how you display it. Without proper support the toy will sag in one direction.

There are two schools of thought on restoration. Some people feel that the toys which have grown old gracefully should remain what they were intended to be, everyday play toys of children from ages past. Only accidentally have they been labeled "collector items." Others maintain that they should be return-

*Schullery, Paul (ed.). *American Bears, Selections from the Writings of Theodore Roosevelt..* Colorado: Colorado Associated University Press, 1983.

ed to their original appearance. Excellent restoration increases the value by at least 25%, and the cost of the repair is but a fraction of this. Maria Schmidt, a specialist in repairing stuffed toys, must be a general practioner too—an all-around ingenious artist. See the Before and After surgery pictures of the 24"/61 cm. champagne mohair (1" long) Teddy Bear given to Rick O'Brien on Christmas morning, 1950. This enterprising child soon "treated" his Teddy to a haircut. After the head was shaved, the bear was put aside in hopes that someday his former beauty could be restored. In 1978 the bear was given to the original owner's son, J. Corey O'Brien, and sent to Maria for restoration.

The most difficult part in repairing this Steiff Teddy Bear was dying the mohair to match. The old fur had lightly faded leaving him with a frosted effect. After she obtained a shade close to the original color (a time cosuming process entailing several hours of mixing dyes and test-dying small swatches) she dyed the fabric. While the fur was still wet, Maria scrubbed off some of the dye to lighten the fur tips. In the end, a close match was achieved. The replaced section appears lighter in the photograph because the nap runs in a direction that reflects the light.

Before restoration. Courtesy J. Corey O'Brien.

After restoration. Courtesy J. Corey O'Brien.

The Status of the Teddy Bear

A case can be made for the democratic status of the Teddy Bear. There have been bears of every size, quality and price so that "every child" could hope to have one of his own. There are those handmade creatures made of scraps from a mother's basket and buttons from her box that are none the less a Teddy Bear.

Many collectors fantasize that a bear is German when the country of origin is unknown. A Teddy Bear is no less lovable nor less interesting historically because it was not made in Germany. The child who loved and played with it contributes to its true value. From its inception, this animated concoction of wool and straw, buttons and cotter pins, has been a loving and well-loved companion to young and old, needy and spoiled. HE IS; therefore he gives; whatever his owner requires of him.

The Teddy Bear was initially a great fad, but unlike other fads, he has survived. For almost a century, the Teddy Bear has been consistently popular and has achieved status as a classic.

II. Teddy Bear Guidelines

Visual Glossary: What to Look For

Knowledge is the key to successful collecting. The following are visual aids to enable one to get a feel for a certain "look" of German (Steiff), American and English Teddy Bears. One must learn to zero in on the clues: Head shape, ear shape, body shape; what makes the bear unique, etc. One can thereby get a handle on Teddy Bear identification. As always, clinical judgment and local experience must be combined with any set of guidelines.

1. Smallish head, wide at the top.
2. Deeply set shoe button eyes.
3. Vertical nose stitched with twisted hard cotton floss. The smaller Steiff Teddies have horizontal noses.
4. Pleasingly pointed long snout.
5. Large hump.
6. Elongated torso, usually twice the length of the head.
7. Long arms extending to the "knees"; paws are curved tapering at the end.
8. Tapered haunches.
9. Extra long feet; the length of feet to the height of bear is a ratio of 1:5.
10. Four embroidered claws; heavy weight felt pads. $100.00-125.00 per inch.

German (Steiff)

American

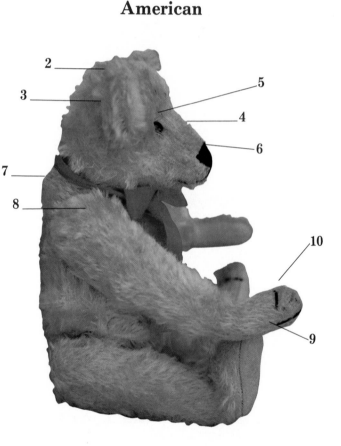

Steiff Teddy Bear (1903-1904); blank button in ear; dark gold mohair, fully jointed by wooden discs; straw stuffed. No attempt has been made in this book to differentiate straw from the fine wood shavings of excelsior.

It is strange that the Ideal Novelty Co. who so responsibly marked their many early dolls and novelty stuffed toys did not label their first Teddy Bears. Since no positive identification has ever been found, the manufacturer can only be "attributed." This 1903-1904 fully jointed, straw stuffed bear has the characteristics considered to be those of the *early* Ideal Teddies.

1. Bright gold mohair.
2. Triangular shape smallish head that is *firmly* stuffed with straw.

6

3. Oversize ears set low on head.
4. Steep forehead with straight jutting snout.
5. Deeply set shoe button eyes. Later eyes could be grey glass/dark pupil.
6. The black nose can be stitched floss or appliqued twill fabric.
7. Smallish hump.
8. Shoulders are set low on torso.
9. When sitting, the longish arms extend over the long pointy feet.
10. Three embroidered claws; triangular-like pads of single weight felt. $50.00 UP per inch.

American

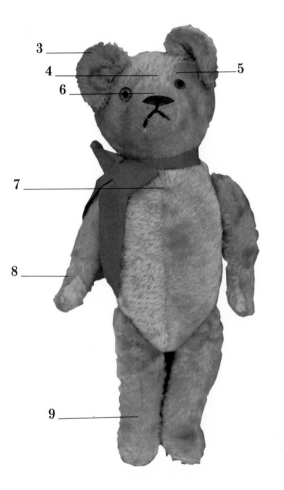

American; unknown manufacturer, ca. 1920; fully jointed by cardboard discs.

1. *Short* pile gold mohair.
2. Entire bear is straw stuffed *extra hard*.
3. Oversize ears.
4. Shorter snout.
5. Glass stick-pin eyes, often with painted backs.
6. Appliqued black or dark brown twill fabric nose; coarse floss mouth.
7. Almost no hump on the long narrow torso, often football-shape.
8. Short straighter arms with little curve to the paw.
9. Skinny straight legs with stubby feet.
10. No claws; *thin* felt pads. $20.00 per inch.

English

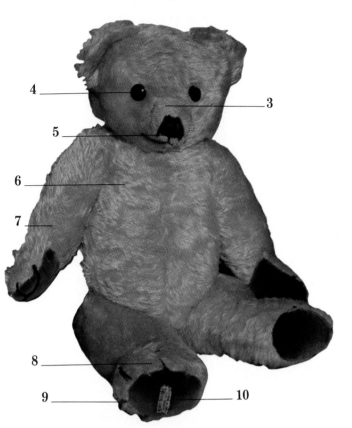

English Teddy Bear, ca. pre-1950s; tagged on the right foot, "Merrythought, Hygienic Toys, Made in England."

1. Long pile gold mohair (manufactured in England).
2. Straw stuffed head; *kapok* stuffed torso/limbs; fully jointed.
3. Large wide head with short, squared-off (pug) snout.
4. Large black flat button-type eyes; glass eyes (often painted on the back) were also used.
5. Widely stitched nose.
6. *Broad shoulders* on a plump torso giving a portly appearance.
7. Shorter arms.
8. *Slim*, well defined ankles.
9. Embroidered claws are found on the more prestigious English Teddies.
10. The teardrop-shape pads can be felt, velveteen, leather or leatherette: but are most commonly a painted oilcloth-type. $20.00-25.00 per inch.

A discussion of the finer value points of early Teddy Bears: The rarest bears in mint condition bring premium prices. These prices are based on age; condition (badly worn bears lose 50% or more of their value); unusual size, color or mechanical performance; I.D.—such as that distinguishing many of the superb Schuco products. When the Steiff ear button is missing from Teddy Bears, other stuffed animals and dolls, the value decreases by 10-25%.

The monetary appreciation of the Teddy Bear is apparent. Overall, fine bears show a 26% annual increase and are expected to show major incremental rises in coming years.

Prices given for Teddies in this book are for *that* particular bear, taking into account its age and/or rarity; condition; unusual features and I.D.

Revised Price Guide Per Inch

Before 1912, *special* Steiff (dark brown or white curly mohair; blank Steiff button; center seam, etc.). $100.00-135.00.

Before 1912, long pile gold mohair, Steiff/button. $75.00 UP.

Before 1912, not Steiff but fine quality (Ideal, Bruin, Bing, etc.). $50.00 UP

Before 1920, mohair, lesser quality but appealing (American). $30.00.

1915-1925, gold bristle mohair, twill nose, skinny legs, short arms (American). $15.00-20.00.

1920-1930, Steiff and other German. $50.00 UP.

Steiff bear or other animal on cast iron or wooden wheels; per inch of *height*. $75.00-100.00.

Steiff bear or other animal on disc wheels/hard rubber tires; per inch of *height*. $27.00.

1920-1930, mohair in unusual colors (pink, red, green, etc.). $20.00-25.00.

1920-1930, cotton plush; no claws. $12.00.

Schuco "Yes/No" Teddy Bears (various periods). $55.00 UP.

1930s, mohair, embroidered or *metal* nose, rounder head, flatter snout (not inset). $15.00 UP.

Made in England, 1930-1950. $20.00-25.00.

Made in England, 1950-1980. $15.00.

European import, finest quality, 1940-1960. $22.00.

"Original Teddy," Steiff/I.D., 1940-1960 (exception miniatures). $25.00-30.00.

"Original Teddy," Steiff, *no I.D.*, 1940-1960 (exception miniatures). $20.00.

"Jackie," Steiff/I.D., commemorating 50 years of Teddy Bears, 1953. $75.00.

"Teddy Baby," Steiff/I.D., 1930s. $90.00.

"Teddy Baby," Steiff/I.D., 1950s. $50.00 UP.

Steiff/I.D., fully jointed "Koala Bear" or "Panda," 1950s. $35.00 UP.

"Zotty," Steiff/I.D., mohair. $15.00.

"Cosy Teddy," Steiff/I.D., 1960s-1970s. $10.00.

Gebr. Hermann, frosted type mohair, 1950-1960. $18.00.

Knickerbocker, Character, Gund, etc., mohair, fully jointed, inset snout, 1930s-1950s. $15.00.

1950s-on, synthetic plush, unjointed. $2.50.

KEY:

f.j. indicates "fully jointed" (swivel head, jointed limbs); disc joints.

I.D. indicates "positive identification."

C.T. indicates "Chest Tag."

N.P.A. indicates "No Price Available."

C.S.P. indicates "Current Sales Price."

1 inch equals 2.54 cm.

III. Margarete Steiff and Her Company

Steiff products appeal to everyone: children, naturalists, artists and collectors. Much of the art is easily recognized. Proof-positive is provided only if it has the famous "Button in Ear." Other toys can be attributed to Steiff through documentation.

Margarete Steiff, a talented Suabian girl from Giengen who was an invalid, made a lasting contribution to the toy/doll world. The greatness of her art and the importance of her contribution is more and more apparent. Her dolls and toys were innovative and original. The dolls were revolutionary for their time, free from the sugary smartness and insipid "dollishness" of the average factory product.

These remarkable dolls with felt heads and a seam down the middle were in production from 1894 to 1930. Their exceptionally large feet/shoes made them the first perfectly balanced, self-supporting doll. The original clothes are extraordinary (and necessary to give high value to the doll today). Designed with simplicity, the doll line included Bavarian children, jovial lads, buxom maidens, policemen, soldiers with equipment, farmers, business persons, carpenters, and dolls of other nations. The caricatures are typified by good-natured exaggeration of features and posture and often comical expressions. These caricatures can be circus performers, mountebanks, German townspeople in gay national costume, village musicians, village schoolmasters, Biliken-types, tea coseys and puppets, and marionettes—all designed by Albert Schlopsnies. Steiff has produced figures of fairytales and legends, and comic strip art, as well as window displays.

The success of the Teddy Bear greatly increased the sale of all the engaging stuffed animals. Today the Margarete Steiff Co. has four factories, two in West Germany (one of which is in Giengen), one in Austria, and one in Tunisia. Note: It is difficult to work with mohair. Mohair is abrasive to the hands. Steiff pays a premium for that labor.

Guidelines and Numbering System

As with any collectible, there seems to be those items that are more rare due to a limited production and being different from the normal line, e.g. the early 1960s bat, lobster, snail and spider. Conversely a fine Steiff toy can be too rare to have created demand, e.g. the floppy nesting hen, ca. 1958. There are more than a few Steiff animals that most serious collectors would like, thereby creating great demand for dinosaurs, fully jointed cats (domestic and wild), costumed animals, moose, "Laika" the Space Dog, "Adebar" the stork, Texas Long Horn, the Lesser Panda, etc. If you are a Steiff collector, you already have Dachshunds, Poodles, penguins, "Jocko," "Slo"

the turtle, "Flossy" fish, squirrels and owls, etc.

How to measure: Do not include the ears or tail. It is simplest to measure the greatest distance—for example, vertical for a sitting animal, horizontal for a lying animal. However, the Steiff Co. usually catalogs by *height*. The yellow ear tag (catalog) numbers must be used with caution. They provide a *general description* of the animal as to pose, material, size, outfit, etc. (see chart on page 10.) Over the years totally different animals could be assigned the same catalog number.

Note, the last two digits *before* the comma or *after* the slash (that appeared in 1968) refer to the size in centimeters. If the number has a slash in it, the three and four position indicate color.

Absolutes of dating are to be avoided. Since catalogs must be photographed early in the year, old stock could be used. Changes in materials and symbols were gradual.

Market trends indicate that collectors are demanding positive identification on Steiff toys, especially those of post-WW II production. When *either* the ear button *or* the chest tag is missing, these collectors prefer to have the chest tag intact; particularly if the animal's pet name is printed. All of the prices listed in the following animal section are based on store new condition, metal button in the ear and paper chest tag.

Revised Chronology Table (Steiff)

Very early years: felt only, shoe button eyes.

1903: mohair introduced.

1903: elephant symbol on paper tag attached to collar or bow.

1903-1904: blank metal button, two prong attachment.

1905: Steiff registered in Germany *Knopf im Ohr* (Button in Ear) trademark.

1905: voice box introduced.

1908: glass eyes introduced.

1905-1950: pewter color metal ear button; *printing* style/ff underscored, two-prong attachment.

1905-1926: *white* I.D. tag attached by ear button.

1927-1950: paper chest tag is a blue bear with a squared off head and a *watermelon mouth*.

1926-1934: *red* (turning to orange) paper I.D. tag attached by ear button.

1940s: cotton/rayon plush used; grey *painted* ear button.

1945-1952: "Made in US-Zone Germany" tag sewn into seam.

1950-1972: blue bear's mouth on paper chest tag changed from watermelon to inverted "V."

1950-1968: shiny metal ear button with *raised script*, still two-prong attachment.

1950s: heyday of Steiff.

1950s: Dralon introduced.

1963-64: last year for glass eyes on Teddy Bears; outer edge is rounded (smooth) on glass, sharp on plastic.

1968-on: comma in I.D. tag changed to *slash*, e.g. 0750/75.

1968-1977: chrome ear button, same flowing script, but *incised*; riveted ca. 1977.

1972-on: paper chest tag changed from yellow/red/blue bear to yellow/red *circle*.

1975-1978-on: change from mohair to synthetics (exception bears, Limited Editions and Collectors Series).

1978-1979: raised script brass button (semi-oval).

1980-on: incised script brass button, riveted; *cloth* I.D. tag replaces paper.

EXPLANATION OF NUMBERS

The numbers show the exact look of the animals as to posture, covering, height in cm and outfit.

Before the line = **series** (kind of animal) **12**/5328,2

After the line
Thousands = Posture

1 - - -	standing	1343,2
2 - - -	lying	2312
3 - - -	sitting	3317
4 - - -	begging	4322
5 - - -	jointed	5322
6 - - -	young	6522
7 - - -	grotesque	7314

Hundreds = Covering

- 1 - -	felt	117
- 3 - -	mohair	3317
- 4 - -	velvet	6412,0
- 5 - -	wool plush	6522
- 6 - -	DRALON Plush	6620
- 8 - -	wood	895
- 9 - -	steel	3980

Tens and Singles = Height in cm

- - 2 2	22 cm high incl. head	1322,0

After the Comma = Outfit

- - - -,0	without wheels	1328,02
- - - -,1	cuddly voice	6328,1
- - - -,2	strong squeeze voice or pull voice of Riding Animals	1328,20
- - - -,3	with Music box	
- - -,ST	Steering	
- - -,ex	on excentric wheels	

Important!

Numbers repeat always therefore please indicate when ordering

Name	or	Series
Foxy 1328,02	or	**26**/1328,02

cm = inches
03 = 1¼
04 = 1½
06 = 2½
07 = 3
08 = 3¼
09 = 3½
10 = 4
12 = 5
14 = 5½
15 = 6
17 = 6½
18 = 6½
19 = 6½
22 = 8½
23 = 8½
25 = 10
28 = 11
35 = 13½
40 = 16
43 = 17
50 = 20
60 = 24
65 = 25½
75 = 29½
80 = 31½
100 = 40

Margarete Steiff GmbH, Feature Catalogue E 1957/58.

IV. Miniature Teddy Bears

The dolls moved out, the bears moved in—to Marlene Wendt's 4-room Bear House, handmade by her including the furniture and fireplace. A Hallmark Santa is behind the tree. Inhabitants are all 3½″/8 cm., made by Schuco and artist Vaneta Smith. It takes imagination with a dash of creativity to enjoy small things. Making and collecting miniatures is a way of escaping the frustrations of the "real world."

Elderly grey-haired: 6″/15 cm., mohair, fully jointed with metal discs, soft cotton and straw stuffed, button-type eyes, black floss nose/mouth, leaf-like ears, extremely long pointed snout, small hump. Suggestive of Billie Possum, a relative of the Teddy Bear, ca. 1910. Maker unknown. Rare. Courtesy Joanna Bruken.

Three Teddy Bears, each 3½″/9cm.: Left, early Steiff button crimped onto ear rim (easily lost); long white mohair, straw stuffed, f.j., black shiny metal eyes, *brown* (Steiff's color for white Teddies) floss nose/mouth; rare small size ca. pre-1912; big feet, long arms, upturned snout. Middle, probably Steiff, no I.D. (thread on chest where paper tag would be); gold mohair, hard stuffed straw, f.j., shiny black eyes, black twisted floss nose; desirable size, cute shape; ca. 1930. Right, probably Steiff ca. 1905, no I.D., gold mohair, hard stuffed straw, f.j., shiny bead type eyes, black twisted floss nose/mouth. Note the large hump for its size, big feet and upturned nose. A rare treasure. Wooden chest, 4″/10 cm. high, 7″/18 cm. long, ca. 1985. All courtesy Marlene Wendt.

Steiff, 3½″/9 cm., very early, very worn; light gold mohair, straw stuffed, f.j., black eyes, *brown* twisted hard cotton floss nose/mouth, no pads on large feet; small hump. The pre-1912 miniature Teddies seem not be found in domestic production. If mint, could triple the value. Courtesy Wanda Loukides.

All bisque (German) bears: 3¼″/8.2 cm., considered animal dolls; made in the early 1900s using the bisque slip left over from dolls; head/torso one piece, wire jointed limbs for versatile posturing; painted features; made in a variety of bear colors, some with molded underwear; size range 2″/5 cm. to 6″/15 cm.; often found damaged since popular play toys. Mint. Courtesy Marlene Wendt.

"Once upon a time there were three bears . . . ," 5″/13 cm., 4″/10 cm., 3″/8 cm., all bisque Papa, Mama and Baby Bear, all marked "Made in Japan," ca. 1920. Courtesy Nan C. Moorehead.

Young owners can add many years to a toy's appearance in a short time. Steiff, 6″/15 cm., pre-WWII, gold mohair, straw stuffed, f.j., glass eyes; well stitched horizontal nose, no claws or pads. Note the desirable upturned snout. Tiny brown pipe cleaner-type dog, ca. 1930. Courtesy Roberta Viscusi.

Different faces on small Teddies: Left, 5″/12.5 cm., gold mohair, straw stuffed, f.j. with wire; black push pin-type eyes; black floss nose/mouth on pointed snout that is clipped to give a distinct expression; no claws or pads. German, ca. 1930s. Center: 4″/10 cm., sparse gold mohair, straw stuffed, rigid neck, wire jointed limbs, amber glass eyes, black stitched nose/mouth, no pads. Note the ears are not hemmed and the 1 piece construction is raveled—cheaply made. Right: 4¾″/12 cm., brown cotton plush with inset snout of woven cloth; swivel head, wire jointed limbs; plastic "stalk" eyes, black stitched nose/mouth; no pads on the woven cloth feet. Maker unknown, ca. 1930; fits into any Teddy Bear collection along with the red metal wagon with wooden wheels. Courtesy Marlene Wendt.

Lesser import quality but old: 6″/15 cm., blue faded to grey mohair, rigid head, arms as well as legs move in unison, straw stuffed, tiny glass "stalk" eyes, black floss nose/mouth, ears *sliced in*, ca. pre-1920. Juvenile book: *Toy Bearkins at School* by John Howard Jewett, printed in Bavaria (1907). The Bearkins series tell of the adventures of the young Teddy Bear. Illustrated in color, they sold for 50¢. Courtesy Ellyn McCorkell.

"Teddy Truckers": Left, "Yorkie" from New York, 8″/20 cm., gold mohair; straw stuffing has begun to settle; f.j., black shoe button eyes, black floss nose/mouth and claws, felt pads; squeaker. Note the unique size with long snout and arms; appealing face. German, pre-1910. Middle, Steiff "Cosy Teddy" look-alike made in Japan: 7″/18 cm., fine textured white synthetic plush (missing the "Cosy" chestplate); hard stuffed straw; wire jointed; amber glass eyes; black *thread* nose ("Cosy" had twisted brown floss); open velvet mouth outlined in black; thin felt pads; ca. 1960. Right, Yes/No "Tricky" bear: 8″/20 cm., high quality beige mohair, hard stuffed straw, f.j., amber glass eyes; black floss (horizontal) nose/mouth and claws; felt pads/cardboard innersoles; squeaker in front torso. Move tail to activate head movement. Schuco ca. 1950. The small size increases value. The competition from the Japanese toy industry (see above) made it difficult for many German firms to maintain their lead in the late 1950s, early 1960s; this contributed to Schuco's demise. Red wooden truck made by Fisher Price. All courtesy Marlene Wendt.

Bear Family came from Canada by way of Japan or Germany: Left, 6"/15 cm., silky blue (unusual color) plush, hard stuffed straw, wire jointed, amber glass eyes; black stitched nose/mouth, ca. 1940. Middle, 5¼"/13.3 cm., gold cotton-type plush, hard stuffed straw, wire jointed, plastic eyes; black floss nose/mouth; original skirt. Right, 6½"/16.5 cm., brown rayon plush, hard stuffed straw, wire jointed limbs, glass eyes, black floss nose/mouth. Owner made two ears out of one for the blue bear missing an ear. Brown bear had no ears; owner made them out of a closely matched plush. Far right, 6½"/16.5 cm., brown short pile synthetic plush covers straw stuffed head, metal body and wire arms; black button-type eyes, black metal nose; metal hands and feet. Key wound to turn 5 metal pages in book picturing cat, dog, duck, hen, pony etc. There is a magnet in the arm causing the pages to turn when touched. Key wound toys are not as collectible as battery-powered toys, ca. 1950. Courtesy Marlene Wendt.

Rare *white* miniature 3½"/9 cm., "Original Teddy," ca. 1950s: Mohair, straw stuffed, f.j., glass bead eyes, brown twisted hard cotton floss nose/mouth, no pads. Excellent investment potential because of demand. Courtesy Wanda Loukides.

Color combinations of old and new: Back, Hermann, 5"/13 cm., black, f.j.; Steiff, 4½"/11 cm., No. 0202/11, beige mohair, posable by bendable wire; Hermann, 6"/15 cm., f.j. gold mohair; Hermann, 5"/13 cm., f.j., tan mohair (53% wool, 47% cotton); Steiff, 5½"/14 cm., No. 0202/14, f.j., caramel mohair. All C.S.P. Front: Clemens, 3"/7.5 cm. f.j., lush white mohair in desirable small size, older; Steiff 4"/10 cm. No. 0201/10, f.j., beige mohair holding 2½"/6 cm., Schuco f.j., gold mohair; next to Steiff, 4"/10 cm., No. 0206/10 f.j., chocolate brown mohair; Steiff, 3½"/9 cm., f.j., lt. caramel mohair from 1950s;, Clemens, 5"/13 cm., f.j., long pile thick white mohair, early 1980s. All courtesy Joanna Bruken.

Left: Musical Teddy, 5″/12.5 cm., pale pink mohair/white mohair snout and pads; glass eyes, brown floss nose/mouth; music box in body plays by turning the handle extending from paw. Unusual infant toy, ca. late 1950s. Maker unknown. Right, 5″/12.5 cm., souvenir of West Berlin; white mohair, wire jointed limbs, stationary head; grey glass pushpin eyes; black thread nose/mouth; red tongue; "Berlin" on chest banner; foil crown, ca. 1960. Courtesy Wanda Loukides.

German, 5½″/14 cm.: Left, prickly beige mohair; right, bright gold mohair with original red ribbon; straw stuffed; cheaply made with plastic brads on outside of jointed limbs, stationary head, no pads, black *thread eyes*, nose and mouth, ca. 1950-1960. Courtesy Wanda Loukides.

Berg, "Animals with Heart," made in Austria: Left, imaginative green creature with antennae, 5″/13 cm., knitted plush, pipe cleaner stem arms and legs, plastic eyes, painted features and inset brown long pile plush hair. Shaggy monkey, 7½″/19 cm., synthetic plush, swivel head, arms and legs jointed by bendable wire, plastic eyes, painted features. The red heart is *securely* attached to chest. Chick, 2½″/6 cm., yellow mohair, hard stuffed cotton, plastic googly eyes, hard plastic beak, felt wings and feet. Duck/bandanna, 2¾″/7 cm., white mohair, sewn on wings, plastic button eyes, felt beak and feet. From original owner who bought them for under $5.00 in late 1960s. Courtesy Susan Roeder.

Life can be a picnic when you share. Teddy Bears' Picnic in the woods, 18"/46 cm. x 20"/51 cm. There is a scene in each corner. *Everyone* has come, even the Circus Bears (with ruffs) from New York. They are having champagne and cake from Fauchon's, Paris, in the upper left corner. Upper right corner: the old Steiff Bear Family, Papa (in plaid vest) is roasting hot dogs. A baby bear is holding a doll that resembles Goldilocks! The basket in center was made with linen thread. Foreground: the Rowdy Bears playing cards on a tree stump. In the 4th corner (not shown) is a Fisherman Bear wanting to join them. This miniaturization is especially animated with many functional accessories. The land (plaster of Paris) is contoured under the moss. There are 22 bears. Courtesy Betsy Gottschalk and Julie Scott.

Wooden Teddy: 4½"/12 cm.; lathe-turned walnut; fur is indicated by the grain; limbs are jointed by cord; ears and nose are peg-fitted; Scandanavian import, ca. late 1960s. Drum is a Christmas tree ornament, 1¼"/3.2 cm., diam. (Author).

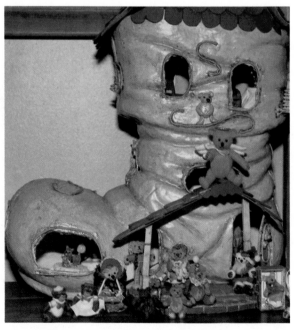

Sold as souvenirs from the Smokey Mountains and elsewhere: 5"/12.5 cm., black or brown synthetic plush, straw stuffed, unjointed, early vinyl snout, glass eyes; red collar/chain, ca. 1960s. For the present, easy to find. Courtesy Roberta Viscusi.

Boot House made by Marlene Wendt. The main boot was a Santa boot used for Christmas crafts. There is a bedroom upstairs and half of the roof lifts up; porch was added. Angel Bear, 3"/7.5 cm., made of felt by Romel Geris. Other Teddies created by Sara Phillips: Bear in Trunk, 1½"/3.8 cm.; Peddler, 1¾"/4.5 cm.; Santa Bear; Compact Bear, green; Perfume Bear, pink (all discontinued).

16

V. Teddy Bears Before 1940

Teddy Bears trimming their feather Christmas tree with other Teddies. The 5 Steiff bears show an assortment of design, color and size during a 10-year period. Clockwise: Rare white Steiff with printed button, 14″/35.5 cm., ca. 1907-1910; center seam Steiff, 23″/58.5 cm., ca. 1905; brown Steiff with printed button, 10″/25 cm., ca. 1906-1908; beige Steiff with printed button, 28″/71 cm., ca. 1907-1910; honey color Steiff with printed button, 20″/51 cm., ca. 1908-1915. Courtesy Barbara Lauver. N.P.A.

Teddy Bears

1903-1912

Steiff with gutta-percha nose: 17″/43 cm., light gold mohair head, paws and feet; jointed arms and swivel neck. The body is two-tone wool plush ("made-on" outfit of gold and red); shoe button eyes; formed nose of gutta-percha (a resin substance resembling rubber from the latex of several Malaysian trees). Exceedingly rare, ca. 1907-1908. Courtesy Beverly Port.

Early Steiff rod bear, 21″/53 cm., jointed with metal rods—hip to hip, shoulder to shoulder—from center of shoulder rod to head. Long silky gold mohair, hard stuffed straw, f.j., large shoe button eyes; originally gutta-percha (gum or resin from a tree) was used for the nose on these exceedingly rare Teddies made such a short time, ca. 1903. The jointing method could not withstand play and the head was easily dislocated. Note also the early pads on the extra long feet. The felt was reinforced with *two* layers, cardboard and black felt. Only a handful of "Rod Bears" are known to exist today. Courtesy Beverly Port.

"Kellie," 23″/58 cm., Steiff with center seam in head gusset, ca. 1905: Honey colored, long curly mohair, straw and kapok stuffed, f.j., shoe button eyes, brown twisted hard cotton floss nose stitched over cloth, 4 claws, felt pads that are reinforced with colored felt, round drum-shaped squeaker. Note broad head and fat (fairly soft) elongated body indicative of the earliest Steiff Teddy Bear. No I.D. A plausible explanation for the center seam in head was to conserve fabric. In the early days (and even later on) when the pattern for a bear was traced near the edge of the mohair, some pieces would not fit. Rather than discard this salvage, the head gusset was placed on the edge and then pieced together with a seam down the middle. Mohair has always been expensive and the frugal Germans would want to get the most bears out of their fabric. Not all center seam bears look alike, some have straight long arms and longer snouts; others have hooked arms and a blunter snout. Extremely rare and highly collectible. Courtesy Barbara Lauver.

Creme de la creme of Steiff: "Tyler," 16"/41 cm., cinnamon (desirable color) mohair, f.j., straw stuffed, shoe button eyes, perfect dark brown twisted hard cotton floss vertical nose/mouth, 4 claws, tan beaver felt pads, long feet, long straight arms, large hump, ca. 1903. No I.D.; mint. Courtesy Maria Schmidt.

The plushness of the white mohair is evident on this fine early Steiff with blank button: 10"/25 cm., straw stuffed, f.j., shoe button eyes, rust color twisted hard cotton floss nose in Margaret Strong style, 4 claws, felt pads, squeaker, ca. 1905. The wooden wheeled skates are added. Courtesy Dot Franklin.

Steiff with blank button: 16″/41 cm., long curly dark gold mohair, straw stuffed, f.j., black shoe button bright eyes; black twisted hard cotton floss nose reinforced with reddish brown felt underneath the stitching—a practical measure for this vulnerable area but only found on the *earliest* Teddies. The 4 claws are defined with the same black floss; felt pads with the feet having cardboard innersoles. Note the wide shape of the head with long nose; long arms with curved paws; elongated feet wih perfect symmetry. A prime example in unplayed-with condition, ca. 1903-1904. Courtesy Diane Hoffman.

"Pearlie," has her own strands of cultured pearls: 16″/40.5 cm., desirable cinnamon color long pile mohair, straw stuffed, f.j., deep set wooden shoe button eyes, dark brown twisted hard cotton floss nose/mouth, 4 claws, felt pads with cardboard innersoles; long feet and arms, beautiful hump. The long snout is accentuated by minimal wear that does not appreciably alter value. Steiff, no I.D., ca. 1904. Courtesy Kelly Tidwell.

Getting ready to start the day; Steiff blank ear button, 14″/36 cm., blonde long pile mohair, dark brown twisted hard cotton floss nose (vertical), mouth and 4 claws. The deeply set shoe button eyes are partially obscured by the long fur; beige felt pads. Note the long arms with the paws reaching to the "knees," longer torso twice the length of the head, and extra long feet, ca. 1904. Mint. The completely outfitted washstand, ca. 1880-1900, is equally a treasure. Courtesy Diane Hoffman.

Steiff: 10″/25 cm., brass color thick mohair, straw and kapok (for easing contours) stuffed, f.j., tiny black shoe button eyes, dark brown twisted hard cotton floss nose/mouth (in Margaret Strong style), 4 claws, original beige felt pads on long slender feet; squeaker. The long snout was slightly clipped at factory, ca. 1903-1905. Beware: The unscrupulous are "instantly aging" the present Steiff reissues. After removing the rivetted button the Teddy Bear is restuffed with fine wood shavings and shaken in a bag with vacuum cleaner dust. Test the fragility of the textile: A needle/thread will not hold well in the old backing. Columbian-type cloth doll, ca. 1900. (Author).

"Otto" with old printed Steiff button: 12″/30.5 cm., lt. gold mohair, f.j., straw stuffed, black shoe button eyes deeply set close together, black floss horizontal nose (now referred to as a "Margaret Strong" type nose), floss mouth and claws, felt pads, long arms and large well-shaped feet, hump and working squeaker. Strikingly similar to the 12″/30 cm., 1904 Margaret Strong Bear. Near mint. Courtesy Dee Hockenberry.

The perennial Steiff: 12″/30 cm., light gold luxurious pile mohair, f.j., dark brown twisted floss (horizontal) nose/mouth, 4 claws; deep set shoe button eyes, beige felt pads, squeaker. Note long arms, 7″/18 cm., and curved paws. Friend same as above but has less settling of the straw stuffing. With time straw loses its explosive quality. Found resting in front of their 28″/71 cm. long (6 wheels) Packard Roadster made by the American National Co. ca. 1927. Courtesy Diane Hoffman.

Blank button Steiff: 9″/23 cm., originally white mohair aged to champagne, all straw, f.j., shoe button eyes, rust floss (horizontal) nose/mouth and 4 claws, felt pads on long *thin* feet; squeaker. The most objectionable site of fur loss is the top of head. Snout and head need a mohair transplant. Use tweezers to take mohair (a *few* hairs at a time) from around joints; tip hairs with Sobo glue; press in with a toothpick, ca. 1904. "Eat at Joe's" (sign missing); metal and plastic wind-up marked "Occupied Japan." Courtesy Diane Hoffman.

"Dustbin"; so named because he was recently recovered from a dustbin in England; 12"/30.5 cm., pale apricot short pile mohair, straw and raw cotton stuffed, replaced shoe button eyes, slightly upturned black floss nose, mouth and claws; long straight arms, felt pads on long feet, slim ankles; some fur loss. Probable Steiff: He appears to be the exact pattern of the 1902-1903 Richard Steiff silver grey. Courtesy Dee Hockenberry.

Richard Steiff 1902-1903 Limited Edition Bear: 12½"/32 cm., No. 0150/32 white cloth I.D. tag attached by large (9 mm. diam.) brass incised Steiff button. Presented in 1983 (12,000 U.S.A., 8,000 Germany). Suggested retail, $90.00. This bear has the potential to esculate in price dramatically. (Author).

TWINS! Originally owned by sibblings, these ca. 1903-1904 Steiffs with blank buttons, are well loved but endure: 17"/43 cm., white and 17"/43 cm., cinnamon, long pile thick mohair, wonderfully conformed: Pointed snouts, long arms, elongated torso, hump, big feet. Brown floss (stitched over cloth) vertical noses/mouth and 4 claws, shoe button eyes, f.j., all straw; original red silk ribbon. These examples of the classic antique Teddy Bear are ribbon winners. This deep cinnamon is a favorite color among the Germans who collect Steiff Teddy Bears. Stroller, wicker and iron, ca. 1900. All courtesy Nan C. Moorehead.

Old Masters Painting: Left, "Daddy's Bear," 20″/51 cm., reddish brown long pile mohair, straw stuffed head, cotton in body and limbs, f.j.; unusual *celluloid* stick pin eyes with bright red pupils and clear irises that were originally painted pink, twisted wool nose/mouth, no claws, soft pads of thin felt or heavy flannel; large ears, elongated pads on paws, feet are stumpy. Note: celluloid eyes are often found on bears of domestic manufacture, ca. 1930s. Raymond J. Schinhofen received this bear from "Santa" Christmas, 1936. The care and feeding of this Teddy Bear has been taken over by his family. Center, 11″/27 cm., Steiff, no button, thread where chest tag was (a *quasi* identification), gold mohair, all straw, f.j., glass eyes, brown floss nose/mouth, 4 claws, yellowish felt pads on long feet (2½″/6 cm.); ears low and flat on head, ca. 1950. Largest and oldest, 22″/56 cm., apricot colored long curly mohair (one can understand why these bears were advertised as "silk plush"); straw stuffed, f.j., large shoe button eyes, vertical nose stitched with twisted hard cotton floss, 4 claws, acutely curved paws, long feet (5″/13 cm.) with double weight beige felt pads and hard innersoles. No. I.D., probable Steiff, ca. 1903. An arbitrary value must be added for his magnificence regardless of manufacturer. Courtesy Mary A. Schinhofen.

Steiff Polar Bear with extraordinary *internal* hinged jointing mechanism of metal within the body and legs. White mohair, 13″/33 cm. long, straw stuffed, shoe button eyes, light brown twisted hard cotton floss nose/mouth and claws; felt pads. Note the extra long feet and small ears as found on the Polar Bear in nature. Beyond the unique jointing method, he is a treasure in his own right, ca. 1908. Courtesy Beverly Port.

TOP LEFT: In the history of the Steiff Co., 1903-1908 are known as the "Bear Years" *(Barenjahre)*. During this time the factory could hardly fulfill the demand for their bears. Steiff, old button "ff" underscored, 13½"/34 cm., f.j., straw stuffed, long pile gold mohair, shoe button eyes closely set giving a cute expression, brown floss nose/mouth and claws, felt pads (left replaced). Courtesy Dee Hockenberry.

TOP RIGHT: Beautiful face: "Eustace," 1986 Workman-Bialosky Calendar bear, 12"/30.5 cm., snow white mohair, f.j., straw stuffed, brown glass eyes, *brown* (found on white bears) floss horizontal nose, mouth and claws, tan felt pads, long arms and feet; hump on this 1912 Steiff with printed button. Mint. Courtesy Dee Hockenberry.

BOTTOM LEFT: Forlorn look that says, "Hold me." Steiff button "ff" underscored, 16"/41 cm., long pile lt. gold mohair, f.j., straw stuffed, deeply set shoe button eyes, black floss (vertical) nose, mouth and claws, long curved arms, long snout, hump, and non-working growler; all typical of the pre-1912 era. Pads were replaced long ago (paws with leather, feet with chamois). However, this does not substantially subtract from value. Courtesy Dee Hockenberry.

"Harry," left: Steiff button "ff" underscored, 18"/46 cm., light cream color mohair, straw stuffed, f.j., black shoe button eyes, black twisted hard cotton floss nose/mouth, 4 claws; original heavy felt pads color matched to mohair. He has long arms and feet and great wisdom. Harry hypnotized owner into buying him. Some wear; ca. 1910. Some wear. Right, "Aunt Maggie" brought from Scotland, ca. 1920s: 19"/48 cm., straw stuffed, f.j.; cinnamon mohair, large black button eyes, black floss nose/mouth (tension on the floss pulls the mouth inward so that upper lip protrudes over lower); replaced pads; long body with a curve in center back producing a hump. Courtesy Jessie "Ted" Casciano.

"Mr. Steiff" and "Crandon" join the circus. Left, 8"/20 cm., pewter Steiff button "ff" underscored, light gold long pile mohair turned greyish with dust and time, straw stuffed, f.j.; the set of the glass eyes gives a cranky expression, black twisted floss nose/mouth, 4 claws, felt pads, squeaker, hump, ca. 1915. "Crandon," 11"/27 cm., beige mohair, straw stuffed, f.j., shoe button eyes, floss nose/mouth and claws, felt pads on large chunky feet, long arms, hump; note the ears are set low on head, ca. 1910. The American "Crandon" is as exciting to the collector as the German "Mr. Steiff." Shown with parts of the Schoenhut "Humpty Dumpty Circus." Courtesy Peggy Young.

Exact dating (1906) from the original owner catapults this fine bear to the front of the continuing parade of Teddies. He is 16"/40.5 cm.; pale gold mohair; straw stuffed (body is softer than limbs); f.j.; deeply set shoe button eyes; brown *velvet inset* nose at end of long snout; brown floss mouth and reddish brown floss claws; *velvet* pads; squeaker. Note the 3"/7.5 cm. long pointy feet, 8"/20 cm. long slender curved arms and large hump. This rare Teddy appears to be identical to the cover and page 86 of Vol. I. Maker unknown. Courtesy Marlene Wendt.

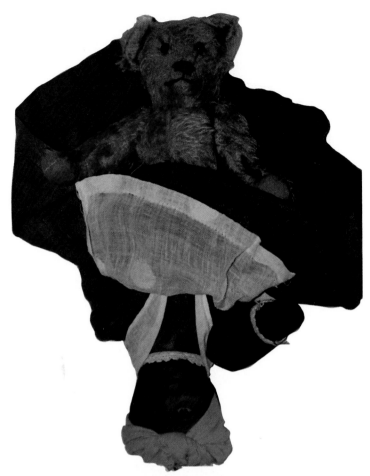

The quizzical, whimsical, "Please pick me up," look of the early (probable) Ideal bear: 14½″/37 cm., thick light gold mohair; straw stuffed, f.j., shoe button eyes deeply set in the wide shape head; black floss nose/mouth and claws; felt pads on *pointy* feet; non-working squeaker, ca. 1912. Courtesy Lisa Osta.

Topsy-Turvy doll combined with a bear figure: 13″/33 cm., gold mohair bear, straw stuffed, jointed head and arms, shoe button eyes, rust floss stitched nose/mouth, cotton flannel pads, original blue cotton skirt. This extremely rare toy made by Dreamland Doll Co., ca. 1907, is further enhanced by the *black* (worth 30% more) Babyland Rag-type doll. An outstanding collector's item today. Courtesy Dot Franklin.

Allie and Fran: Left, 11½″/29 cm., gold mohair, straw stuffed, f.j., shoe button eyes, black floss nose/mouth and 3 claws, felt pads, voice box, hump. Note the small ears. Maker unknown, ca. 1912. Fran, right: 12″/30.5 cm., long pile gold mohair, straw stuffed, f.j., shoe button eyes deeply set close together, black floss nose/mouth and claws, felt pads on extra long arms and feet, squeaker, hump. Note the extremely long (clipped) snout in wide head. Maker unknown, ca. 1910. A most attractive bear and must be valued equal to a tagged Steiff. Courtesy Kelly Tidwell.

Arnold and Amanda have become dear friends. Even though she is "on-in-years", she is a bit of a flirt winning his heart from first they met. Arnold: 13"/33 cm., honey color mohair, straw stuffed, f.j.; glass eyes are *grey* with a black pupil (often found on early Ideal Teddy Bears); black floss nose/mouth and claws, felt pads, long curved arms, long feet, large ears are well to the side of head, large hump. Ideal, ca. pre-1910. Mint. Amanda, 12"/30.5 cm., light honey color mohair, straw stuffed, f.j., shoe button eyes; upturned nose is black floss, stitched claws, replaced felt pads on longish feet, long arms; maker unknown, ca. 1915. She wears a pink chiffon dress and old lace hat; she insists on one pearl earring for her left ear. Courtesy Jessie "Ted" Casciano.

Drummer Boy bear: 22"/56 cm., gold mohair, hard stuffed with *cork* (unusual), *wood* disc joints, amber glass eyes, black floss nose/mouth, claws, felt pads, hump, long curved arms and big feet, ca. pre-1912. This great bear has a drum worthy of him: Wood, 9"/23 cm. diam.; lithographed designs of The Roosevelt Bears in hunting and military outifts, ca. 1910. Courtesy Marlene Wendt.

In need of help, one brown bear injured in a dog fight: 16"/41 cm., gold mohair, f.j., shoe button eyes replaced with glass; original brown cloth nose with *black floss overstitching* on long snout; 5 floss claws on long feet, curved paws. Note the black *horsehair* stuffing exposed in arm; it combines with straw in torso. Steiff never used animal hair or sawdust for stuffing material. If one is not experienced in extensive restoration, they should seek skilled help. Good repair increases the value at least 25%. In the meantime, he is loved for inner beauty—not outward appearance. American (slightly shorter arms), pre-1912. Courtesy Diane Hoffman.

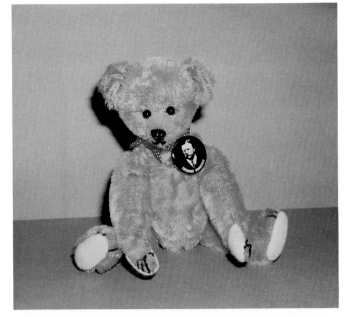

Probably Ideal Teddy Bear, ca. 1910: Gold mohair, 14″/35.5 cm., straw stuffed, f.j., black shoe button eyes, black floss nose/mouth, claws, repaired tan felt pads on big pointy feet, long arms, hump. Note the sewn features and placement of eyes and ears on the wide head creates "mood." Courtesy Dee Hockenberry.

Early unmarked Ideal: 12″/30 cm., short thick gold mohair, f.j., straw stuffed, floss nose/mouth and claws, shoe button eyes, felt pads replaced to exact specifications, hump. Note the triangular shaped face of an Ideal bear—the larger low set ears, the extremely deep-set shoe button eyes, and a *steep* forehead with a straight jutting snout. This pre-1912 Ideal bear has lasted because of the superior quality and is underpriced at this time because of lack of positive identification (pedigree). Courtesy Maria Schmidt.

The popularity of American Teddy Bears is seen in this photo postcard (postmarked "1908, Kewanee, Ill."). The bears could be Ideal or Bruin, etc. (Author).

Around 1910, Teddy Bears were made in large quanitites by many manufacturers in several countries. Unknown maker: 19″/48 cm., off-white mohair, straw stuffed, f.j., clear glass eyes, vertical floss nose/mouth, 4 claws (Steiff Teddy Bears are found with 4 stitched claws, but other makes also have 4 claws). Note the long snout and arms; huge feet. Slightly worn condition but unique. Courtesy Gwen Daniel.

The accompanying photographs from original owner give exact dating (1908): 24″/61 cm., high quality off-white mohair, straw stuffed, f.j., glass eyes (the paint has worn off of the backs making them appear clear), floss nose/mouth and claws, felt pads, working growler, original bow. Maker unknown. The large size and white color enhance value. Courtesy Lisa Osta.

Bruin Mfg. Co. of New York: 13″/33 cm., honey gold mohair, straw stuffed, f.j., wooden shoe button eyes, black floss nose (worn), mouth and claws, beige felt pads on pointy feet, hump. Note the low shoulders typical of some Bruin Teddy Bears. On the right foot pad, there is a discernible wide band where the "B.M.C." cloth tag once was. Memorize this face and the distinctive set of the ears. These fine early American bears are underpriced today, ca. 1907. Courtesy Wanda Loukides.

Homemade, ca. 1910: 17″/43 cm., black knobby upholstery fabric, straw stuffed, string jointed arms and legs, head sewn on; eyes are old metal edged pearl buttons; tan floss nose/mouth; old tan leather gloves having decorative stitching are used for pads; long (9″/23 cm.) curved arms; body is pouch-shaped; the look of hair set with curlers. Courtesy Marlene Wendt.

American Teddy Bear: 22″/56 cm., short golden mohair, straw stuffed, f.j., glass eyes, embroidered nose/mouth, felt pads, small squeaker in the back, hump. Note the football-shaped body and perfectly *round* head that is appealing to many collectors. From original owner, ca. 1910. Courtesy Barbara Lauver.

A creative expression of a Teddy Bear: 18″/46 cm., black velour, handcrafted with love, ca. 1910; bone button eyes, red sewn nose, big ears, "stick" arms and legs support his fat body; all stuffed with sawdust; original silk ribbon. This is an important bear, historically and aesthetically (the essence of great modern design is minimalism). These early primitive examples are avidly sought along with cloth dolls. Turn-of-the-century stroller, iron and heavy coated fabric. Courtesy Nan C. Moorehead.

Large standing bear toy as animal; 14½″/37 cm. tall, 21″/53 cm. long, rust color mohair, straw stuffed, unjointed, glass eyes, floss nose/mouth; bearlike appearance with hump, thick haunches and small tail. These bears on all fours (he *never* had wheels) are not commanding the high prices that they should, ca. 1910. Mint. Courtesy Nan C. Moorehead.

Early conformation: 10″/25 cm., light gold mohair, straw stuffed with kapok cradling squeaker, f.j., deep set shoe button eyes, black floss nose/mouth, 4 claws, felt pads, long arms, small head and ears. Maker unknown, ca. pre-1912. Courtesy Rosemary Moran.

Teddy Bears 1912-1920

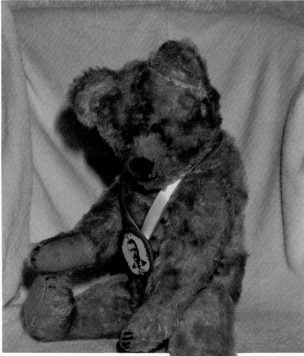

Bear with panache: "Rosie," 16″/41 cm., *apricot* colored mohair, all straw stuffed, f.j., black shoe button bright eyes, floss nose/mouth, 4 claws; felt pads. Probable Steiff. Very good condition. Courtesy Gwen Daniels.

"Doc," 20″/51 cm., long pile dark gold mohair, f.j., straw stuffed, shoe button eyes, floss nose/mouth and claws, felt pads, growler; long curved arms, large feet, hump. High quality large Teddy Bear; maker unknown, ca. 1912. Near mint. Courtesy Linda K. Lilley.

American, ca. 1915: 9½″/24 cm., light gold mohair, straw stuffed, f.j., vertical black floss nose/mouth, 4 claws, tiny glass eyes, felt pads on shorter arms and thicker feet. There is no positive I.D. for this often seen snout and bear. They are bargains, albeit the fur is easily matted. *All leather* dolls, 10″/25 cm., painted and molded faces in comic expression, separate ears, glued on human hair, wool broadcloth outfits, ca. 1920; an example of attention to detail typical of the era. Courtesy Rosemary Moran.

"Bruin," Farnell Alpha Teddy Bear: 18"/46 cm., beige mohair, straw stuffed, f.j., deep set glass eyes with airbrushed markings, black heavy floss nose/mouth, gravity-type voice box (also found in early dolls), long arms and feet. Value wise: Personality plus cancels out wear. J.K. Farnell was one of the few English firms making "German Style" Teddy Bears. The high quality of the early Farnell toys must be seen to be appreciated, ca. 1915. Contrasting to lesser quality, brown burlap, 10"/25 cm., straw stuffed, f.j., sliced-in ears, shoe button eyes, stitched nose/mouth and claws; possibly homemade (if adeptly done it is hard to tell), ca. pre-1920. Courtesy Rosemary Moran.

Gold medium pile mohair, 20"/51 cm., hard stuffed straw, f.j., shoe button eyes, black *yarn* horizontal nose, 3 claws on long (3½"/9 cm.) thicker feet; nicely curved arms; long pronounced snout; tilt-type voice box. Studying variations in nose stitching (if original) can be a rewarding key to identification. Some wear. Maker unknown, ca. pre-1920. Courtesy Nancy Catlin.

"I can hold this pose forever": 27"/68.5 cm., gold bristle mohair, hard stuffed straw, f.j., shoe button eyes, black floss nose/mouth in life-like style, claws, tan twill pads, hump, long snout (some wear), long legs. American, pre-1920. Courtesy Dee Hockenberry.

Beautifully dressed child, Jessie "Ted" Casciano, with her Teddy Bear, 1915 exactly. Two reasons for the Teddy Bear hobby: Some say, "I started because I never had any as a child." Others say, "One collects Teddy Bears because they HAD them as a child." She falls into the latter category.

Early American soft furry bearskin for the child's heart and the collector's eye: 12″/30.5 cm., golden brown mohair, stuffed with straw that has settled to a cuddly softness, f.j., original shoe button eyes; black stitched nose and mouth, the perky smile is a function of the mouth embroidery. On other old bears, sometimes the stitch joining nose to mouth breaks causing the mouth to droop thereby creating a "smile." The felt pads were repaired long ago; 4 floss claws; well-contoured legs with long feet; arms extend to crotch; longish snout on the small head. This model of Teddy crops up often enough to know that it was widely distributed, ca. 1912. He is giving a lesson on *The Three Bears* copyrighted 1923 by Sam'l Gabriel Sons & Co. In 1932 F.A.O. Schwarz sold this book for $.75 to accompany a dressed set of *The Three Bear Family*. Courtesy Mary Alice Carey.

Teddy Bears listen to our secrets, share our concerns, give wise counsel and cheer us on. Bright gold mohair, 22″/56 cm., firmly straw stuffed, f.j., glass eyes; thick black floss horizontal nose/mouth, 5 claws, felt pads. Note the big ears and large size typical of this mint American Teddy, ca. pre-1920. Edith Doll, 21″/53 cm., adapted from Dare Wright's book, *The Lonely Doll*. Rothschild Doll Co., 1985. Courtesy; Rosemary Moran.

Collectors have an intensely personal attachment to their Teddy Bears; attested to by the names given them making each a family member. Boonie's gentle manner make him an excellent companion for the prim and proper Cricket. "Boonie," 19″/48 cm., golden brown mohair, straw stuffed, f.j., glass eyes replace unmatched buttons, black *twill* nose; original mouth is heavy *red* embroidery cord, long straight body, long legs, short arms with tips reaching hips, felt pads, growler. The large ears suggest Ideal, ca. 1920. The most popular clothes for Teddy Bears are: Sailor; clown; suit and vests. Courtesy Jessie "Ted" Casciano.

"Cricket," 16½″/42 cm., gold long pile mohair with a dark brown backing; called "two tone"; usually fur and backing is color-matched; f.j., views the world through black shoe button eyes, black floss nose (side to side), no claws, old black velvet replaces original pads. After much coaxing, she removed her dress, but NOT her bloomers, to show her straw stuffed body. "Cricket" is a prim bear and proud of her antique straw hat. Maker unknown, ca. 1915. Courtesy Jessie "Ted" Casciano.

"Here I am, come and love me": 26″/66 cm, gold thick pile short mohair, straw stuffed, f.j., grey and black glass eyes, long snout with black twill nose suggests Ideal, ca. pre-1920. Many Ideal bears of this era had twill noses, but not every twill nose belonged to an Ideal Teddy Bear. Ears are wide set, gathered at base rather than set on bias; felt pads, hump, fat body. Courtesy Joanna Brunken.

"Babysitting can be a bore": 22″/56 cm., thinning gold mohair, straw stuffed, f.j., amber glass eyes, black twill nose, floss mouth, no claws, original kid leather pads, large hump. American, ca. 1915. Shown with 14″/36 cm., black composition Scootles doll. Courtesy Peggy Young.

Thinking of the days of wine and roses: 20″/51 cm., gold short pile mohair, straw stuffed, f.j., black shoe button eyes, floss nose/mouth and claws, felt pads replaced with cloth; large hump, nicely curved shorter arms, long snout. American, pre-1920. Pony Express wagon, 35″/89 cm., wood spoke wheels, ca. 1915. Courtesy Peggy Young.

Peaceful: Left, 18″/46 cm., long pile burnished gold mohair; straw stuffed; short arms and large head are disc jointed, unjointed legs in a sitting position, brown glass eyes, black stitched nose, felt pads. He houses a music box that when wound plays *Rosalie*. Musical Teddies were most popular in the 1930s. This is an unusual example. Right, in chair: 22″/56 cm., long pile beige mohair, straw stuffed, f.j., black shoe button eyes, black stitched nose/mouth, felt pads on large paws and feet. A squeaker provides his voice; uncommon large bear, ca. 1920. Courtesy Dot Franklin.

Two examples of the doll as bear, showing the readiness of doll manufacturers to take advantage of the Teddy Bear craze: Left, 12½"/32 cm., short gold mohair, celluloid face, hard stuffed straw, wire joints at shoulders and hips only; white felt mittens and boots, inoperable voice box, crack in face, ca. 1914. Right: 11"/29 cm., red short mohair with bisque head, straw stuffed, f.j., blue glass eyes, felt pads, squeaker; removable red mohair pointed hood. These novelties are in no more demand today than they were in 1914. Courtesy Marlene Wendt.

"Nifty," 22"/56 cm., glacier blue-grey long pile mohair, (unusual color and large size); straw stuffed, f.j., dark *red* glass eyes with black pupil (the painted back has faded); stitched floss nose; long ago the original felt pads were replaced with beaver fur; voice box. Note the long tapered snout and long feet on this high quality American-made bear. Purchased in 1916 at McHugh Hardware Store, Bellingham WA by owner's father, J.P. Nelson. The early Teddies in seldom seen colors are prized today. Some wear. Courtesy Margaret N. Rea.

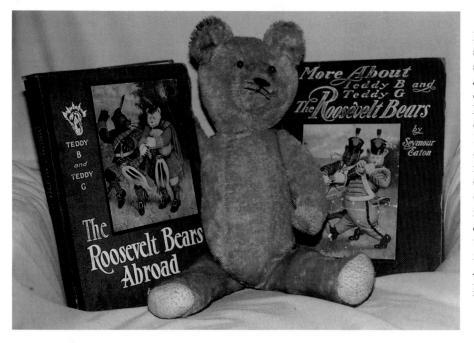

Reading about his "forebears": 19"/48 cm., short gold mohair, hard stuffed straw, f.j., shoe button eyes, *brown twill* nose *double mouth* stitched with brown floss (unusual); off-white felt pads, squeaker high in back; hump; the longish snout is askew from years of play. Excellent condition. Attributed to Ideal, ca. 1915. Books, 8½"/22 cm. x 11"/28 cm., hard bound by Seymour Eaton (pen name of Paul Piper), illustrated by R.K. Culver and copyrighted by Edward Stern & Co., Inc. Left, *The Roosevelt Bears Abroad* is the third and best (1907); More About *Teddy B and Teddy G The Roosevelt Bears* is the second and hardest to find (1908). The fourth and last of this first series is *The Bear Detectives* (1908). For top value, all color plates must be intact. Courtesy Marlene Wendt.

Large bears show to advantage. They are eye-catchers. Snow white mohair, 30"/76 cm., straw hard stuffed, f.j., black floss vertical nose, mouth, no claws; glass eyes, large ears and thick feet, original twill pads have been replaced. Note the gusset in arm pattern. In a long arm, this enables a curve. American, ca. pre-1920. Add extra value for white. Courtesy Joanna Brunken.

The first day of school and not too happy about it, "Lord D'Arcy": 17"/43 cm., gold mohair with a green cast; straw stuffed; f.j.; yellow and black glass eyes; resewn nose/mouth, no claws; replaced pads; hump. The resewn effort often adds personality, American, pre-1920. "Felix the Cat" school supply case dated 1933. Courtesy Peggy Young.

Left: German, ca. early 1900s, 6"/15 cm. tall, 8½"/22 cm. long, pale gold mohair, straw hard stuffed, unjointed (wire in legs) deep set shoe button eyes, no pads, black floss nose/mouth. Note: Ears sewn close to head and forward. Right: Steiff Panda, standing, 3"/8 cm. high, 6"/15 cm. long, white and black mohair, straw stuffed, swivel head, glass eyes, felt pads, black floss nose. Complete with ear button, red collar and bell, ca. late 1950s. Desirable small size. Courtesy Marlene Wendt.

Teddy Bears 1912-1920

American: 20″/51 cm., gold matted mohair, firmly straw stuffed, f.j., glass eyes, black twill nose, floss mouth, no claws on stubby feet with bright gold felt pads, arms reach to hips; note the folded ears, ca. pre-1920. Pet dog: 10″/25 cm., long soft coat (mohair) of the Pekingese, straw stuffed, f.j., replaced eyes, mended pug nose, long flat tail as seen in 1934 Steiff catalogue. No I.D. Courtesy Diane Hoffman.

Bright gold mohair: 8″/20 cm., straw stuffed, f.j., amber glass eyes, black floss nose ("side to side") and mouth, cream color felt pads on paws only; non-working squeaker. Unknown maker, ca. 1920. Courtesy Wanda Loukides.

Electric-eye Teddy Bear with switch in left ear: 26″/66 cm., gold mohair, straw stuffed, f.j., light bulb eyes, horizontal floss nose/mouth, no claws, felt pads. Electric-eye Teddy Bears appear to be of only domestic production, a novelty, ca. 1915. Some wear. Spic and Span, 8½″/22 cm., wind-up made by Louis Marx, ca. 1920. Courtesy Diane Hoffman.

Teddy Bears 1920-1930

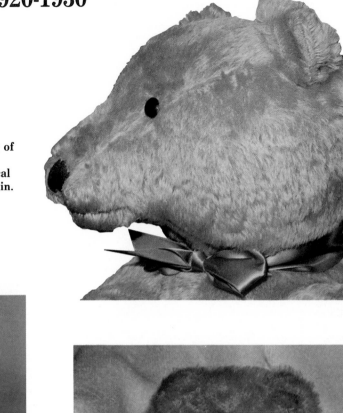

A face with definition: 1922 Steiff in pristine condition. Note the sculpting of the head; the large shoe button eyes; black hard cotton twisted floss vertical nose; the mouth floss parallels the chin. 26″/66 cm.

English Teddy Bear purchased on Portabello Rd.: 21½″/55 cm., grey mohair, straw stuffed (settling from upper arms), f.j., clear glass eyes painted light blue on back, black floss nose/mouth and claws, tan felt pads (cardboard innersoles); long curved arms with big paws; *round* face accentuated by the unusual original placement of ears (sewn into seam at front and sliced in for the rest). There are instances where English firms (as well as Japanese and some German) sliced the head to insert the ears, ca. 1920. Add value for excellent condition, grey color and unusual appeal. Courtesy Dee Hockenberry.

Unknown maker: 12″/30.5 cm., gold mohair, straw stuffed, f.j., one glass eye, floss nose/mouth, no claws; felt pads, long feet, long curved arms; squeaker. Popular child-size Teddy, ca. 1920. Some wear. Repro T.R. button. Note that Teddy Bears over 14″/36 cm. command the premium prices. Courtesy Linda K. Lilley.

41

The wedding of Theodora and Theodore: each is 20½"/52 cm., gold mohair, hard stuffed straw, f.j., amber glass eyes, floss nose/mouth, felt pads on long skinny legs, short arms, ca. 1920. The preacher, "Rev. Sherman Horntoot," is a new Teddy Bear belonging to Mark Steele, New Zealand. There is a growing nucleus of Teddy Bear collectors in Australia and New Zealand. Courtesy Peggy Young.

"Peter," 14"/36 cm., frosted brown mohair and a mechanical head give a nature-like appearance. Paper chest tag reads, "Peter, Ges gesch. Nr. 895257." The self-recognizable head is mohair covered papier mache. When the head is turned, the black and white wooden eyes roll; at the same time, the tongue moves from side to side in the open mouth/teeth. The body is similar to other Teddy Bear bodies made by Gebruder Sussen-guth, ca. 1925: straw stuffed, f.j., felt pads. This novelty was also made in gold frosted black and with glass googly eyes. The original box is an enhancement and one of the few instances where a Teddy Bear box is obtainable. Though costly now; it will prove a good investment. Mint. Courtesy Dee Hockenberry.

Bear family has stayed together: Papa, 17½"/44 cm.; Mama, 13"/33 cm., Baby, 10"/25 cm., gold sparse/bristle mohair, f.j., straw *hard* stuffed, amber glass eyes, gold (thin) felt pads, fabric twill nose, squeakers. All have the same features: short arms, slender body, *long* legs, not much snout. This species of bear is NOT popular with most collectors and should not be valued highly. However, these American Teddy Bears charm some collectors who buy them for their age, not their appearance. Teddy Bears have great fur or horrid fur. Many 1920s bears have horrid fur unlike the next generation where we once again find long pile thick mohair, e.g. Knickerbocker, Character, etc. Courtesy Marlene Wendt.

"Socks," 14"/36 cm., bristly gold mohair, hard stuffed straw, f.j. (arm joints sewn down and never repaired); glass eyes replaced with shoe buttons, floss nose/mouth, old doll socks tied over remnants of felt pads, skinny limbs. A good example of an American bear produced in quantity to meet the demands of a bear-hungry generation, ca. 1920. Rocking horse: 25"/64 cm. high, brown burlap covered wood body padded with straw, carved head and legs, glass eyes, horsehair mane and tail, red painted wood rockers, pewter stirrups; velvet covered cardboard/cloth saddle; bridle, missing reins, ca. 1915. Courtesy Peggy Young.

"Murf" proves that beauty is only fur deep; 12"/30 cm., f.j., gold mohair, straw stuffed; neither shoe button eye appears to be original nor do they match; mouth replaced and set in a stoic smile; hardly any feet and thin arms with patch upon patch on the pads. Not the finest of bears but a true charmer. American, ca. 1920-1930. Courtesy Carolyn Dockray.

Germans call this a *Glokenspiel* Teddy Bear: 18"/46 cm., long pile gold mohair, blonde tips, f.j., straw stuffed, *very large* original glass eyes, black floss nose (crescent shaped) embroidered to perfection, 4 claws, felt pads on long feet, unique ear treatment. There is a concertina inside body: The squeeze-operated music box (plays like an accordian) produces a beautiful bell-like sound. The oversize eyes seem to be found only on the soft toys (including dogs and cats) that have a squeeze-type music box. Purported to be made by the Helvetic Co. The Teddy Bears usually have a special color of mohair covering, e.g. yellow, pink, green, etc. and are lightly frosted. This example was purchased at F.A.O. Schwarz, New York in 1925. Mint. Courtesy Sammie Chambliss.

Patchwork Teddy Bear; 11½″/29 cm., various wool fabrics in grey tones, arms and legs wire jointed, head stationary, straw stuffed, amber glass eyes; black thread nose and mouth; green wool foot pads and ear linings, ca. 1920s. Determining the age of homemade stuffed toys is difficult; there is less documentation. This bear follows the trend of patchwork quilting popular during the '20s. Courtesy Wanda Loukides.

"Vernon," 18″/46 cm., worn gold mohair, hard stuffed straw, f.j., amber glass eyes, black floss nose, pads redone in black fabric, long thin body and legs, short arms as seen in American manufacture, ca. 1920. The faded overalls are hand sewn with love and original to him. Courtesy Wanda Loukides.

German, probable Gebr. Sussenguth, 24″/61 cm., long pile brown tipped mohair, f.j., straw stuffed, glass eyes, floss nose (side to side), mouth and 3 claws; working music box plays slowly; felt pads repadded. Note that the ears and snout are a bit different. Excellent condition, ca. late 1920s. Courtesy Gwen Daniel.

Old honey bear: 19″/48 cm., greyed honey color mohair, straw stuffed, f.j., glass eyes, floss nose (side to side), mouth and claws, felt pads, inset long snout, big floppy ears, fat tummy, small hump, growler. Note the *round* head and thicker feet. German, unknown maker ca. 1925-1930. Courtesy Sammie Chambliss.

Marching Bear: 22″/56 cm., unjointed, gold plush head, cotton stuffed head, torso and arms, straw stuffed legs, yellow flannel hands; glass eyes, missing brown cotton pompon nose; embroidered mouth, cardboard innersoles; made-to-body red felt outfit with brass buttons and rayon trimmings. Note the *huge* ears and the made-to-head cotton stuffed red felt hat with straw plume. An eye catching addition to a Teddy Bear collection. Rare in this fine condition. American, ca. 1925. Courtesy Peggy Young.

It all adds up to value: Bear, 24″/61 cm., gold cotton plush; stuffing is early reprocessed cotton supported with straw; f.j., glass eyes, twisted floss (vertical) nose, no claws; white felt pads, squeaker. American, ca. 1930. There is little demand for old *cotton* plush toys: It collects soil, is easily matted and does not appeal to the tactile sense. "Maxi," 4½″/12 cm., No. 2180/12, new C.T., made in Austria; black and grey inset mohair, double weight orange felt nose, nylon whiskers, white felt feet and digging claws; tail. "Maxi" is one of the last miniature animals that Steiff made of mohair. Very common. Courtesy Diane Hoffman.

45

"Petsy," 1928 Steiff, pewter ear button "ff" underscored: 14"/35.5 cm., two-tone cream color mohair tipped with cinnamon brown, head is straw stuffed, body/limbs straw and kapok, f.j.; the distinguishing original blue eyes appear to be button-type rather than stick pin; *reddish* brown heavy twisted cotton floss nose (horizontal), mouth and claws, felt pads on elongated feet, long curved arms— much the conformation of earlier Steiff Teddy Bears. During these times there was not the worry of turning over inventory, so the company stuck with what was successful. This is indeed a most unusual and rare bear of any age. Courtesy Betty DiBattista.

Drum major: 23"/58 cm. (including hat), gold plush head, hard stuffed straw, unjointed, glass eyes, black floss nose/mouth; made-to-body red flannel pants, blue jacket and hat, ca. 1920. The haughty expression implies at least 76 trombones in his band. A blue ribbon winner, Calif., 1980. Courtesy Marlene Wendt.

Steiff "Teddy Clown" bear, ca. 1928: 18"/46 cm., curly white mohair mottled with brown (vestiges at joints and inside ears), f.j., softly straw stuffed, *large* brown glass eyes, twisted hard cotton black floss vertical nose (the smaller sizes had horizontal stitched nose), felt pads, 4 claws; long arms, big feet and hump; all characteristics of earlier Steiff bears as well. There is no evidence that he ever had ruff and hat (decorated with either red or blue pom-poms). Perhaps the larger version of this rare Steiff never had the sewn-on outfit. It does not alter his value. The 12½"/32 cm. size was reproduced as a Limited Edition for 1986. Courtesy Maria Schmidt.

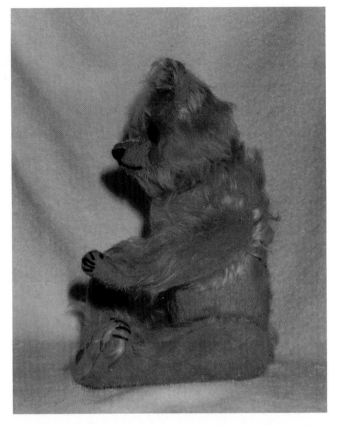

Mechanical *and* musical German clown bear: 20½"/52 cm., luxurious mohair: Lavender head, one arm and half front body; pale green arm and half front body; pink leg and half back body; gold leg and half back body. All colors except gold have paled but this does not alter the value of this *very* rare Teddy Bear. Straw stuffed, clear glass eyes (suggestive of Schuco and other German manufacturers), original light pink wool felt pads. Nose is med. brown floss; mouth is unusual (red floss with center worked in a button hole stitch to resemble a lip); ears are large and unstuffed, long arms with slightly curved paws, long feet. Fully jointed by wood discs; highly unusual neck construction; three large wood discs have a square hole in center through which a square peg passes. This allows his head to move from side to side and also nod up and down. When you nod his head, a lovely chime-like music box is activated. A treasure from the late 1920s in all original condition. Courtesy Jessie "Ted" Casciano.

Teddy Bear with oversize eyes attributed to the Helvetic Co.: 12"/30.5 cm., pink and beige long pile mohair, f.j., straw stuffed, floss nose/mouth, 4 claws, felt pads on long feet, nicely shaped curved paws; the legs and torso are the same length. The distinguishing feature is the paper squeeze-type music box producing beautiful music. From original owner, late 1920s. Worn condition. Courtesy Linda K. Lilley.

Curious expression: "German" bear, 16"/40 cm., light gold mohair, f.j., straw stuffed, clear glass eyes (KERSA is one German company that used clear glass eyes), horizontal black floss nose/3 claws, felt pads replaced. He is proportioned in the German fashion: Longer torso with hump, long straight arms and big feet. He has an old type growler found in early Steiff Teddy Bears. Excellent condition, ca. 1920s. Courtesy Maria Schmidt.

"Squeaker," 9″/23 cm., sparse gold mohair on *pink* backing, straw stuffed, f.j., black glass bead eyes, floss nose/mouth, *sliced-in* ears, gold felt pads. Cheaper craftsmanship, ca. 1920-1930. Heavy metal train made by Keystone, ca. 1930. Courtesy Diane Hoffman.

"Poor Fred," 18″/46 cm., gold long pile mohair frosted brown, f.j., *hard* stuffed straw, glass eyes, love-worn stitched nose, *wide head, short arms,* velveteen pads, *pointy feet,* growler. All to indicate probable American, late 1920s. Courtesy Roberta Viscusi.

Gold mohair frosted in browns: 10″/25 cm., straw stuffed, f.j., brown glass eyes, black floss nose/mouth; snout and pads are beige mohair; squeaker. Probable Gebr. Hermann: Either the 1927 model (reissued in 1986), or a similar bear appearing with the Gebr. Hermann tag, ca. 1960. Courtesy Wanda Loukides.

"Hot - Cha," 10″/25 cm., black long pile mohair, f.j., kapok stuffed body/limbs; head is stuffed with straw and a thousand secrets; shiny glass eyes (stick pin-type); flashing pink-orange *silk* floss nose/mouth; cream color felt pads; squeaker. A true friend to original owner since 1929; a strong little Teddy Bear. Value must be added for the rare black color seldom used because it could appear threatening to the child. Courtesy Jessie "Ted" Casciano.

Teddy Bears 1930-1940

A bear's best friend is his boy: Johnnie and Joanie are typical children of the 1930s. The Teddy Bear was a baby gift, Sept. 1930. He was the popular 13"/33 cm. size with chocolate brown long fur; large button eyes and long jointed limbs. Dearly loved for many years; hair has worn thin and growler is quiet. Note the four playthings in photo: Doll, Kiddie Car, chair and Teddy Bear. Courtesy Virginia Joy.

To compliment other Teddy Bears in your collection: 16"/40.5 cm., burnished gold long pile mohair, all straw stuffed, f.j., small eyes with worn painted backing appearing clear now; black floss nose/mouth, 3 claws, felt pads on pointy feet. Press tummy to activate a music box (adds value). Note the broad head with flat crown. American, ca. 1930. Many Teddy Bears were made in this average size. Courtesy Rosemary Moran.

Waiting for his porridge: 13"/33 cm., extra long light gold silky mohair, softly stuffed with straw, f.j., *clear* glass eyes, black stitched nose/mouth and claws, felt pads, squeaker in tummy. The *small* ears, close-set eyes and worn snout give a vulnerable baby look, ca. 1930. Add value for this special appeal and the high quality. Unknown maker. Courtesy Marlene Wendt.

"Bearly Pink," 20″/51 cm., pink shaggy mohair, straw stuffed, f.j., glass eyes, floss nose/mouth and claws, replaced felt pads; some wear on snout vulnerable to a child's play. Many people collect by topic—for example: pink. American, ca. 1930. Riding "bear back" on platform horse, 42″/106.5 cm.; carved wood head and legs; horse hide covering and mane; straw stuffed; glass eyes; saddle missing, ca. pre-1920. Courtesy Peggy Young.

"Tasi" is a "gentlebear" who won't tell his age: 19½″/50 cm., long pale gold mohair, f.j., head hard stuffed straw, body/limbs kapok; wide set glass eyes give him a "knowing look"; black floss nose/mouth, no claws, tan felt pads. He does need his glasses for doing puzzles and reading. American, ca. 1930. Courtesy Jessie "Ted" Casciano.

The horse back rider: 14″/35.5 cm., golden mohair musical Teddy Bear of 1930s; plays "Rock-a-bye Baby" in beautiful tones; glass eyes, velveteen pads; f.j.. Pony: 19″/48 cm. high, 25″/64 cm. long, spotted brown/white mohair, all straw stuffed, glass eyes, horsehair mane/tail; original trappings. There is no sign that he ever had wheels; the pewter Steiff button "ff" underscored (used until late 1940s) has also been found on a white pony with wooden wheels. Courtesy Nancy Crane.

Sledding party: Bear, 13"/33 cm., long pile beige mohair, sheared mohair inset snout, straw and soft stuffed, f.j., glass eyes, floss nose/mouth and claws; the pads are of an early quality velveteen; Teddy has just enough wear to give character yet hold value. American, ca. 1930. "Renny," reindeer: 8½"/22 cm. high, No. 1322,00 (also made in 5½"/14 cm. size); silky beige mohair spotted brown, straw stuffed, brown glass eyes, black twisted floss nose with a single white horizontal "highlight" stitch (frequently used by Steiff); felt horns/bendable wire armature; non-working squeaker, ca. 1965. Hard to find and popular. Courtesy Nancy Crane.

A lecture from Prof. Bear: 13"/33 cm., long rust mohair, straw/kapok stuffed, f.j., tin decal eyes, floss nose/mouth, no claws, sheared mohair long inset snout, velveteen pads, growler; short curved arms, well-shaped long legs. American ca. 1930. Add value for fur color, unusual eyes and mint condition. Courtesy Roberta Viscusi.

Father and son: Left, 7"/18 cm., champagne mohair, straw stuffed, f.j., glass eyes, black floss horizontal nose, 3 claws, inset snout, cotton flannel pads, squeaker, excellent condition, ca. early 1930s. A later version of the 1908 "Laughing Bear": 14"/36 cm., shaggy champagne mohair, straw stuffed, f.j., glass eyes, black floss horizontal nose, 3 claws, inset snout with open mouth, hard sole feet with original cotton flannel pads. Good condition, maker unknown, ca. early 1930s. All courtesy Maria Schmidt.

51

Teddy Bears 1930-1940

Oversize head: 23″/58 cm., grey thick high quality mohair, hard stuffed straw head, soft stuffed body/limbs, f.j., large amber glass eyes, floss nose/mouth, no claws, felt pads, curvy arms; American, ca. 1930, playing with his tin and hard rubber toys of the same era. Courtesy Peggy Young.

Known Steiff Teddies from 1935-1940 are rare. These vintage bears show the last of the distinctive qualities prized as "early Steiff": small head in relation to a longer torso; long snout; long arms with curved paws; long feet on tapered legs; hump. Pewter color printed button "ff" underscored, remnants of *yellow* I.D. tag: 13½″/35 cm., No. 5335,2, gold mohair, straw stuffed, f.j., glass eyes, twisted hard cotton floss nose/mouth, 4 claws; heavy weight felt pads, non-working squeaker. Mint. Courtesy Lisa Osta.

A frolic of bears: Left, 9″/23 cm., a "Cheeky" look-alike; orange/gold plush, gold velveteen snout, straw and soft stuffed, jointed arms and legs only, glass eyes, black molded plastic nose, black painted mouth; maroon velveteen pads, ca. 1975, made in Taiwan. Girl, 9″/23 cm., gold mohair, hard stuffed straw head, body/limbs soft, f.j.; long ago the original glass eyes were replaced with shoe buttons; black floss stitched nose (side to side); felt pads, inoperable squeaker; well loved childhood Teddy Bear of owner; a Christmas present 1934. Courtesy Joanna Brunken.

"Rosamond," 36"/91.5 cm., rose colored long curly mohair, f.j., straw stuffed, amber glass eyes, black floss nose/mouth and claws, tan felt pads, hump. English (possible Twyford), ca. 1930. Her head is so heavy that it sags forward (which adds to her charm). She is the only girl in the den and given her size, the other bears look up to her. Near mint. Courtesy Dee Hockenberry.

Lady Bear, from England of course, attending an important exhibit of 1930s Bavarian art prints by Austrian artist Ida Bohatta. Milady is 17"/43 cm. tall, ca. 1930; luxurious blonde mohair, head is straw stuffed, body soft; glass eyes, floss nose, painted fabric pads; antique mink coat and hat. Courtesy Nan C. Moorehead.

English charm: 17"/43 cm., light gold medium pile mohair, straw stuffed head, kapok stuffed torso/limbs; glass eyes; floss nose/mouth, 4 stitched claws; teardrop-shape light brown painted oilcloth pads; slim ankles and wrists. Note the *upward* strokes on the stitched nose (a technique used by Merrythought today) and the unusual head shape, ca. 1930. Purchased in England. (Author).

In spite of his size, this 29″/74 cm. English toy has the "bear-ing" of a baby, a spoiled one at that. Rust color cotton plush is well loved but unbroken, f.j., straw stuffed, painted fabric pads, stick-pin glass eyes, resewn nose and mouth, floppy ears, well-shaped arms and legs with defined ankles, working growler, ca. 1930. Courtesy Nan C. Moorehead.

English (Chad Valley) and German (Steiff): 26″/66 cm., thick gold mohair; straw stuffed head, straw and kapok torso, kapok limbs; black floss nose/mouth and claws; amber glass eyes, tan canvas pads; tag sewn on left pad: "Hygenic Toys Made in England by Chad Valley." Note that after 1938 the stitched-to-foot tag read: "The Chad Valley Co., Ltd., by appointment Toy Makers to H.M. Queen Elizabeth, The Queen Mother." Extraordinary giant bear, ca. 1930s. Steiff, 19″/48 cm., gold long pile mohair, straw stuffed, f.j., glass eyes, black twisted floss nose/mouth and claws; beige double weight felt pads; growler (tilt-type); C.T. and button; 1940s, early 1950s look.

Late 1930s sleep eye Teddy: 14″/36 cm., rust color cotton plush with contrasting ear linings; white cotton pom-pom nose. The most interesting feature is his open/close painted inset eyes (ball and socket type). With various modifications this eye was used ca. 1920-1940. The yarn pom-pom nose indicates American.

Honey color mohair, curly and long: 21"/53 cm.; straw and kapok stuffed to be soft and cuddly. The *clear* glass eyes and the nose stitched with *upward* points remind one of Merrythought; felt pads on large feet. The appropriate clothes are not original. This wonderful armful is in excellent condition and equal to Steiff quality of the same period, ca. 1930. Courtesy Gwen Daniel.

Japan: 11"/28 cm., sparse gold mohair easily dislodged from backing, straw stuffed, wire jointed; tiny glass eyes, thread nose/mouth, skinny stiff limbs with thin felt pads on arms only, squeaker; original green bow. Store display fuzzy duck, 8"/20 cm., hard rubber covered with long plush. Both ca. 1930-1940. Courtesy Peggy Young.

Robert Louis Stevenson said, "A friend is a present you give yourself." Friend: Rabbit, 17"/43 cm. with ears; early composition head and ears; painted features, comic pie-shape eyes; flange jointed head; straw stuffed muslin torso/limbs jointed by metal discs on the outside; original clothes missing, ca. 1930. Teddy Bear: 12"/30.5 cm., brown long pile mohair with a gold cast; straw stuffed head, cotton stuffed body/limbs, f.j., molded *tin nose* (only found during late 1930s); floss mouth; glass eyes; beige felt pads; stubby feet; no claws; squeaker. Note the rounded head and wonderful large ears. Slight wear on the snout. Courtesy Rosemary Moran.

1938 New York World's Fair souvenir Panda sold near the rare animals who were visiting from China for the first time. Sitting: 9"/23 cm., black and white plush, reprocessed cotton stuffed, swivel head; limbs jointed by bendable wire armature enabling him to stand on all fours; amber glass stick pin eyes on the black plush patches; black thread nose/mouth, red felt tongue; white velveteen pads; white tail; squeaker. The exact dating and historical significance increases value. From original owner, Jessie "Ted" Casciano.

The Great Steiff classic, Teddy Baby from the 1930s: 6"/15 cm., light gold mohair, straw stuffed, f.j., glass eyes, twisted hard cotton floss nose, open mouth; long *velvet* snout, downward turned paws on longer arms; *velvet* feet; non-working squeaker. Bow replaces the original leather collar/bell; old printed button "ff" underscored. The rare miniature size increases value. Courtesy Dee Hockenberry.

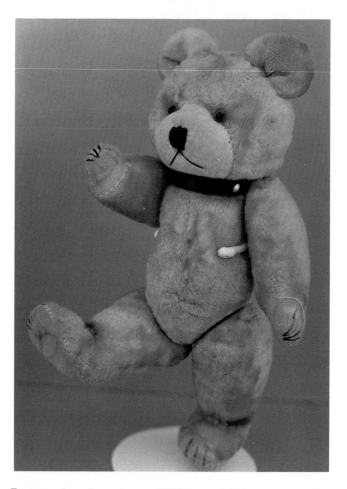

Rayon velour from Japan: 8"/20 cm., tightly straw stuffed, f.j., inset snout; *sliced in* ears; glass eyes; *thread* nose/mouth; 4 stitched claws on decorated pads; original collar with rivet closure. Ca. 1930. Courtesy Rosemary Moran.

"Francesca" the bear: 18"/46 cm., natural tan lambskin, hard stuffed wool, f.j., large bright orange glass eyes, leather nose/mouth, black leather pads. Note the perfect heart shape formed by head and ears. Lamb's fleece bears were popular ca. 1930-40; the skins deteriorate and they are often found in poor condition. Courtesy Roberta Viscusi. Mint.

VI. Teddy Bears, 1940 - Present

Teddy Bears 1940-1960

Steiff, 21″/53 cm., golden curly mohair that looks like cotton candy; straw stuffed, f.j.; glass eyes; twisted floss nose/mouth, four claws; felt pads on superb long feet; hump; growler. Note that the early Steiff features of long snout, long arms, etc. are evident on this ca. 1940 Teddy Bear purchased in West Berlin. For some time, German collectors have been enthusiastic participants in the Teddy Bear field. This noteworthy bear holds a colorful book, *Dear Old Verses.* Courtesy Claudia Shotwell.

Distinguished Steiff bear adds an important dimension to a Teddy Bear collection: 12″/30.5 cm.; cinnamon color dense *cotton plush*; straw stuffed, f.j.; beautiful glass eyes; black cotton twisted floss (horizontal) nose/mouth, four claws; cream color felt pads. Note the long straight arms (6″/15 cm.). These cotton plush Teddies made such a short time during the war years are very rare today. Taking no chances, the early printed Steiff button "ff" underscored is secured with scotch tape. Mint. Courtesy "Sweetie" Whitson.

Waiting for a blanket party: 16½″/42 cm., long pile white mohair, straw and cotton stuffed, f.j., amber glass eyes, black floss nose, mouth; no claws ('40s bears usually had no claws); felt pads, voice box. Note, the clipped face and snout delineates the wistful expression. Exact dating from original owner, 1941. Courtesy Joanna Brunken.

Googly Teddy valentine hugs Steiff bears: Left, 8½"/22 cm., gold mohair, hard stuffed straw, f.j., glass eyes; black twisted floss (vertical) nose/mouth, 4 claws; felt pads; small hump; squeaker; ear button. A popular size, ca. early 1950s. Right: 6"/15 cm., same as above but no pads on the pointed feet; button, ca. early 1950s. Valentine with stand: Movable eyes are flat glass discs glued into cutout spaces, early 1900s. Courtesy Marlene Wendt.

Humanized, denoted by long legs: 25"/64 cm., brown and gold cotton plush, clothes sewn as body, inset painted vinyl snout, circular flatish head, glass eyes/felt backing (also made with celluloid disc eyes), *short* curved arms; all suggestive of a circus bear. The hard stuffed cotton legs make him self-standing, unjointed. For the Teddy Bear historian: Few examples of this minimally produced bear are found, but his rarity has not created demand. American, ca. WW II years. Courtesy Brenda Hoyle.

Bear Boy, 10"/25 cm., dark brown synthetic plush, composition face. Original chest tag, "Swiss made." There is no substitute for original identification, ca. 1940. Courtesy Nan C. Moorehead.

"Great Bear": 28″/71 cm., grizzly dark grey-black 1″/2.5 cm. long mohair, f.j., cotton stuffed, glass eyes, floss nose/mouth (red is the color usually used on black bears), no claws, velveteen pads (repadded), large hump, 2 growlers (front and back). He survived a fire; was cleaned and repadded (fortunate for the historic perspective). Probable Knickerbocker, ca. 1940s.

"I'll look after you.": 28″/71 cm., ca. 1930 American brown bear, probable Knickerbocker; f.j., head straw stuffed, body soft; mohair is rich brown with a greenish cast, sheared brown mohair snout, glass eyes, floss nose/mouth, no claws, tan velveteen pads. Long blonde mohair, 14″/36 cm., sheared blonde inset snout (a characteristic of Hermann), glass button eyes, floss nose/mouth and 3 *claws* (typically Hermann), lt. tan felt pads, f.j., soft and sawdust stuffed throughout, ca. 1950. Tagged, "Hermann Original Teddy." Courtesy Nan C. Moorehead.

Knickerbocker, 24″/61 cm. (the large size is *not* rare for this company), chocolate brown finest quality mohair; straw head, cotton stuffed torso/limbs, f.j.; brown celluloid eyes, floss (vertical) nose/mouth, velveteen ear linings, snout and pads (all characteristic of Knickerbocker in the 1940s). "Clemens, West Germany," tagged 9″/23 cm., white mohair with self fabric vest, unjointed, open mouth, original blue rayon ribbon and triangular metal "Clemens" tag more recently replaced with a paper triangle. On an unmarked specimen it is difficult to differentiate: Clemens, Hermann, Grisly and Petz. Note the pads are mohair, often found with several of these companies, ca. 1960. All courtesy Diane Hoffman.

Big headed bear: "Jennifer," 20″/51 cm., f.j., thick gold mohair, black shoe button-type eyes, stitched nose/mouth and claws, velveteen pads and inset snout; large round head and floppy ears typical of the 1940s. Add value for size and personality. Courtesy Roberta Viscusi.

Cinnamon Bear: 20″/51 cm., long pile thick mohair, cotton stuffed, f.j., glass eyes; clipped snout (*not* inset); reworked floss nose; no claws; felt pads. As usual, the "Character" tag is stitched into left ear seam, ca. 1940. This high quality Teddy with his vibrant coat should be in greater demand than current sales indicate. Courtesy Ellyn McCorkell.

"Twyford Product, Made in England, Action Toycraft Ltd., London W.3." Without looking at the above label, the bright red felt original pads indicate this Teddy Bear is a "Twyford," ca. 1960. 12½″/31 cm., gold mohair, f.j., straw stuffed head, body and limbs cotton stuffed; plastic eyes, black embroidered nose (vertical) and mouth, red rayon bow; sold in the yellow cotton flannel nightie. Courtesy Joanna Brunken.

Original "Character" tags: All American bears; these handsome examples can proudly bear the flag: 20"/51 cm., ca. 1940, fine quality short pile rust mohair, f.j., head and limbs firmly soft stuffed, torso straw and soft stuffed; shoe button eyes with white felt backing, sewn nose and mouth, replaced felt pads. "Cub," 5"/13 cm. high, 6"/15 cm. long, jointed head only, tan mohair, felt pads with airbrushed claws; other features as above, circa 1960. Courtesy Nan C. Moorehead.

An old stone farmhouse on a Highland Pony Farm in Scotland is home for this medium size, fully jointed Teddy. Acquired by the original owner as a child in Australia; a probable import from the United Kingdom, ca. late 1930s. Note that the shaggy soft mohair retains its luminescent gold color. Courtesy McArdle Family.

"Twyford" tagged 15½"/39 cm. gold mohair, f.j., straw and kapok stuffed, glass stickpin eyes, black floss (vertical) nose and mouth, oilcloth pads, growler. Excellent condition, ca. 1930s. Mint, 20"/51 cm., dense pile white mohair, f.j., kapok stuffed, orange plastic eyes, lt. pink floss nose (vertical) and mouth, the distinctive red felt "Twyford" pads, growler. A handsome bear from ca. late 1950s. Courtesy Maria Schmidt.

"Kiss the cook and eat the cookies": 11″/28 cm., grey-brown high quality mohair, straw stuffed, f.j., glass eyes, floss nose/mouth and claws, felt pads, nonworking squeaker; good conformation on this German (non Steiff) Teddy, ca. 1950s. When this species of bear is found, they are usually small: 10″/25 cm. to 16″/40.5 cm. Cast iron stove, ca. 1900 (reproduced in some sizes). Courtesy Nancy Crane.

Musical: 14″/35.5 cm., thick gold mohair; straw stuffed head and torso, reprocessed cotton limbs; glass eyes; well done black floss nose/mouth; orangish thin felt pads (paw pads an unusual shape), stubby feet. Push the head down and turn to play "Teddy Bears' Picnic." Probably Swiss made by Mutzli, ca. 1950. Schuco miniature, 2½″/6.3 cm., gold mohair Teddy Bear. Courtesy Diane Hoffman.

Undeniably English; maker unknown, 17″/43 cm., gold mohair, f.j., straw stuffed head, straw/kapok body, vertical black floss nose (pug), glass eyes, painted oil cloth pads. Note the wide head, short arms, plump body, *slim ankles*; all characteristic of English bears. The most easily defined trait is the pug nose, ca. 1950. Courtesy Linda Cron.

Steiff Teddy Bear Family from 1950s to mid 1960s: All are mohair, straw stuffed and fully jointed. The 3½"/9 cm. and 6"/15 cm. sizes have no pads; the 7"/18 cm. size has felt pads on back feet *only*. All other sizes have felt pads on *front* and back feet. The 7" and larger have embroidered claws. Care must be taken when measuring a bear. Teddies catalogued as the same size can vary as much as an inch; they are, after all, handmade. Top: 16"/40.5 cm., No. 5340,2; gold mohair, glass eyes, black floss nose, loud squeaker (appears to be a replacement), raised script button. 2nd row: 13½"/35 cm., No. 5335,2; gold mohair, plastic eyes, black floss nose, non-working squeaker; ribbon not original; 10"/25 cm., No. 5325,2; gold mohair, glass eyes, black floss nose, non-working squeaker, original ribbon, appealing expression; 8½"/22 cm., No. 5322,2; gold mohair, glass eyes, black floss nose, non-working squeaker, ribbon not original. 3rd row: 7"/18 cm., No. 5318; *caramel* mohair, *glass* eyes, *brown* floss nose, non-working squeaker; 6"/15 cm., No. 5315; caramel mohair, *plastic* eyes, brown floss nose, raised script button, original ribbon; 7"/18 cm., No. 5318; caramel mohair, *plastic* eyes, brown floss nose; squeaker; note felt pads on back feet *only*; this is a hard-to-find size. Bottom row: All are 3½"/10 cm.; all have No. 5310; all have glass eyes; the gold have *black* floss noses; the 2 center caramel Teddies have *brown* floss noses. This smallest size is avidly sought; the caramel color is also desirable. Research on the "Original Teddy" has proven that in 1965 or 1966 the "long-fur-on-the-nose" variety was changed to the shaved snout. Additionally, *glass* eyes were changed to *plastic* in 1963 or 1964. Courtesy Kirk Stines.

A favorite of young and old alike: In 1953 the Ideal Toy Co. received permission to manufacture this first issue of Smokey the Bear in the likeness of the *U.S.D.A. Forest Service* poster: 14"/36 cm., rust color plush body/limbs, vinyl painted head, hands and feet, cotton stuffed, glassene eyes. The toy did not withstand play due to the wired-on head, hands and feet. It was on the market only a few months; replaced by the vinyl face, plush head number two (see Vol. I, pg. 178). This rare example is missing levis, belt/buckle, badge and shovel. The first issue of anything usually becomes the most valuable. Courtesy Sammie Chambliss.

These two Steiff "bear" out the axiom, "Good as gold." Gold mohair, 13"/33 cm., straw stuffed, f.j., glass eyes, floss nose/mouth, 4 claws; slight hump, longish arms; sloped snout with tight cheek formation; well defined oval feet with felt pads; ca. 1950; no I.D. Shorter gold mohair, 6"/15 cm., straw stuffed, f.j., glass eyes, black floss nose/mouth; note the well shaped snout, haunches and feet on this small size, ca. 1950. Front: Old tin bear on wheels. Courtesy Nan C. Moorehead.

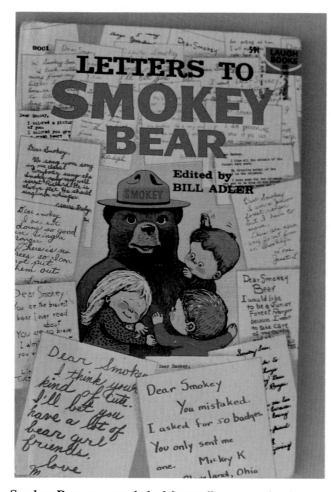

Smokey Bear as a symbol of forest fire prevention became a much beloved national hero to American children as attested to by the compiled letters in the 1966 book edited by Bill Adler and published by Wonder Books, New York, a division of Grosset & Dunlap, Inc. (Author).

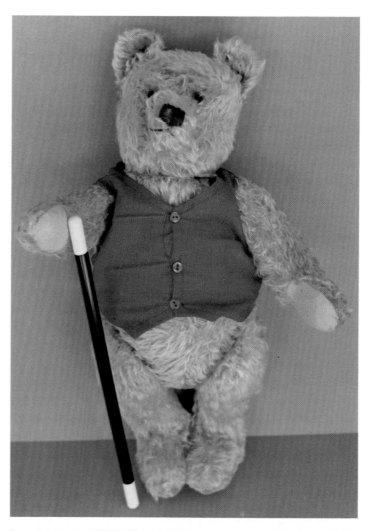

Reminiscent of W.C. Fields: 20"/51 cm., long curly beige mohair, all straw, f.j., dark brown twisted floss nose (vertical)/mouth, 4 claws; fur same length over entire face, glass eyes, double weight felt pads, well-shaped long feet; strong growler. Probable Steiff, ca. 1950. (Author).

Character faces molded in vinyl: Large, 17″/43 cm., sitting, black and white plush cat resembling a panda, vinyl head/painted features; well modelled feet; sweet look, 1950 exactly. Fads change, trends continue and the trend is for these high quality vinyl faced American-made toys to be overlooked as collectibles and priced accordingly. Smaller, tagged "Ideal, recommended by 'Miss Francis' Ding Dong School," 14″/36 cm., tan and cream plush, sleep eyes/tin eyelids and bristle eyelashes, ca. 1955. Courtesy Chris McWilliams.

Steiff, squared-off face beginning in the late '50s, early '60s: 13″/33 cm., gold mohair, firmly straw stuffed, f.j., glass eyes, black twisted floss nose/mouth, 4 claws; heavy weight felt pads; hint of a hump; squeaker. The bear in nature (baby shape) is modified: Straighter arms, legs still shapely but with shorter feet; the intelligent face has a slightly shorter snout. It is not any *one* feature but the composite of the whole that shows change. A number of these high quality examples exist because Steiff's production was at its zenith. The dollar was strong throughout the world and the Americans had pent-up buying power left over from WW II. Courtesy Mary Alice Carey.

Knickerbocker Toy Co., Inc., New York: Pouting Teddy Bear, 15″/38 cm., brown plush body (also made in other colors), soft stuffed, unjointed, painted vinyl face and ears, closed eyes. Collectors are not yet paying for the high quality and modelling warranted by these vinyl faced Teddy Bears, ca. 1955. Courtesy Kay Bransky.

Steiff "Music Teddy," 13½"/35 cm. (one size only), No. 9335,3, long pile gold mohair (59% wool, 41% cotton); straw stuffed, f.j., glass eyes, dark brown twisted floss nose (vertical)/mouth and claws; heavy weight felt pads. When this rare bear is found, the felt circle with "Music" is usually missing. Squeeze the circle to activate the Swiss music box. A chimpanzee also had this feature. Teddy is tagged under the arm, "Made in US-Zone Germany," ca. 1950. This highly prized collectible had a short production period. Mint. Courtesy Chris McWilliams.

Teddy Bear: 8½"/22 cm., white long pile mohair, all straw stuffed, f.j., glass eyes, tan floss nose/mouth, no claws, light pink felt pads, longish feet; squeaker. Note the large triangular head. Purchased in West Berlin; a high quality toy by an unknown maker, ca. 1950. Giraffe: 13½"/35 cm., spotted mohair, straw stuffed, black plastic eyes, airbrushed facial features, mohair horns, pink felt-lined ears; squeaker; raised script button, 1965-1967. Requiring greater workmanship, the open mouth models are generally more popular. Courtesy Claudia Shotwell.

Ideal: 10"/25 cm. high, 18½"/47 cm. long, white cotton plush, hard stuffed cotton, unjointed, legs supported with wire armature, glass eyes, velveteen nose and pads; open mouth with rubber teeth. Tagged, ca. 1950s. White color and positive I.D. increase value. Courtesy Jennifer Sisty.

Koala bears sold as souvenirs in Australia and New Zealand: 9″/23 cm. and 6″/15 cm. sitting; kangaroo fur (plentiful); hard stuffed with wool; glass eyes; leather nose and cut-out feet. *The Bears of Koala Park* by William Pene du Bois; a story about true friendship gloriously illustrated by the author. (Author).

Fifties Steiff bears are increasingly popular: 10½″/27 cm., gold mohair, all straw stuffed, f.j., glass eyes, brown twisted hard cotton floss nose (vertical), mouth and 4 claws, double weight felt pads on longish feet (2¼″/8 cm.); arms mounted high on body give a pleasing profile. Altering the size alters the appearance. On this small bear note the slope of the snout not found on larger Steiff bears of the same period. No I.D. but self-recognizable, ca. 1950. Courtesy Carolyn Altfather.

The fully jointed Steiff "Koala Bear" is as popular as his Teddy Bear cousin and much harder to find. Left, 8½″/22 cm. tall, No. 5322 (also made fully jointed in the more rare 13½″/35 cm. size); light gold long pile mohair, straw stuffed, glass eyes, grey felt nose, sheared mohair paws with separate thumbs; ca. late 1950s. Miniature, 5″/12 cm., jointed head only, (see Vol. I, pg. 185). Courtesy Robin Lowe.

Only in examining the range of sizes can one appreciate the full scope of Steiff animals. Polar Bears standing on all fours: 5"/12.5 cm., No. 1312,0; 6½"/17 cm., No. 1317, 02; large, 10"/25 cm. high, No. 1325, 02; white mohair, straw stuffed, jointed head only; blue leather collar with bell. The smallest has black shoe button-type eyes; the two largest have blue eyes and a strong squeeze voice. The two smallest sizes are relatively common while the largest size is hard to find (true of most Steiff animals), ca. 1950-1960. Courtesy Jane L. Viprino.

Attention is focused on "Teddy Baby," one of the all time favorites of every collector because of his lovable personality: 8½"/22 cm., No. 7322,2 (the second smallest of 4 sizes); brown mohair, sheared tan mohair inset long snout and foot top; straw stuffed, f.j., glass eyes, black twisted hard cotton floss nose and 4 claws; open felt mouth with airbrushed tongue; felt pads/cardboard innersoles for standing. He was reissued in 1984. A "reissue" is made with the exact old style materials in exactly the same manner. In 1985 the tan version appeared and was gone by 1986. This mint example with old C.T. and raised script button dates from early to late 1950s. "Jocko," 19½"/50 cm., brown long pile curly mohair, straw stuffed, f.j., glass eyes; light peach felt face, ears and hands; stitched fingers and separate thumb; the partially open mouth can hold an object. "Jocko" as chimp is a staple of the Steiff Co. His desirable old printed button/ff underscored increases value, ca. before 1950. Courtesy Diane Hoffman.

American Panda: 12"/30.5 cm., black and white mohair; straw stuffed head, soft stuffed torso and limbs; f.j., plastic eyes (note the early use of plastic eyes), floss nose, felt pads; squeaker, ca. 1940-1950; he has a large head, thin arms and the remnants of a tag under right arm. Giant Pandas are now considered close relatives of and in the same family as the bears. This can be extrapolated to Teddy Bears. Courtesy Kirk Stines.

German Teddy: 17"/43 cm., pinkish brown frosted curly plush, inset beige mohair snout and ear linings; straw stuffed rock-hard, f.j.; glass eyes; black floss nose/mouth, no claws; felt pads. The thinner torso and limbs suggest Gebr. Hermann, ca. 1950s. However, other German bears also have sheared mohair ear linings. Steiff "Cosy Blanko" dog: 8½"/22 cm., No. 5060/22, Dralon, synthetic fiber stuffed, jointed head only, glass eyes, open felt mouth, black twisted floss nose stitched with downward points; stitched claws, acrylic pads, ca. 1969. Attractive, but no demand unless one collects Samoyeds. Courtesy Diane Hoffman.

"Ideal Toy Corp. Hollis 23, N.Y., Made in Japan"; 12"/30.5 cm., light strawberry blonde mohair with white mohair inset snout; straw stuffed head, cotton stuffed torso/limbs; f.j.; brown glass eyes; plastic molded nose; pink velveteen open mouth; short arms; burgundy markings painted on pink velveteen pads; 3 black embroidery floss claws. The bell is sewn to chest on the spot where a Steiff tag would be; original pink rayon bow. This high quality *tagged* Teddy Bear should not be overlooked, ca. 1950. Courtesy Bill Gardner.

Teddy Bears 1940-1960

Kamar Co., Japan: 9"/23 cm., straw and cotton stuffed, f.j., cotton and wool blend plush (mohair), brown/black glass eyes, hard plastic molded nose, floss mouth, painted plush pads, squeaker. Clipping the snout gives good detail, ca. 1960. Velveteen dog, 6"/15 cm., cotton stuffed, glass eyes, floss nose, satin-lined ears. Recent import from the Far East. Courtesy Kelly Tidwell.

Hard-to-find Steiff Pandas: Slight variations are found due to size differences; both date from early 1950s-early 1960s. Left, 6"/15 cm., No. 5315; 8½"/22 cm., No. 5322,2; mohair, straw stuffed, f.j., glass eyes; black twisted floss nose; open mouth (velvet on smaller, felt on larger); grey suede-like pads (larger has cardboard innersoles and shaved mohair on tops of feet); larger has non-working squeaker; smaller has raised script button; also made in 13½"/35 cm. and 20"/50 cm. sizes. Value increases logarithmically with size. Courtesy Kirk Stines.

Large Panda: 18"/46 cm., black and white medium pile mohair; hard stuffed cotton/straw, f.j., orange celluloid-type plastic eyes, black floss nose/mouth on typical English snub nose, practical leatherette pads in tear drop shape; elongated head rather than moon face Panda shape; short arms, defined ankles; unknown English or American maker; manufactured from the same pattern used for golden bears. The English companies altered their designs less over the years than other firms, ca. 1950.

Teddy Bears 1960-1980

Rare WHITE "Zotty": 11″/28 cm., No. 6328,02, shaggy white mohair, straw stuffed, f.j., glass eyes, twisted floss (vertical) nose, open felt mouth, felt pads on big feet; squeaker; original ribbon. This appealing example, ca. 1960, would be more difficult to replace than a ca. 1910 Steiff Teddy. Shown with Christmas postcard (also rare). Vintage Steiff postcards are fun to collect and far cheaper than the toys. Courtesy Kirk Stines.

Four Steiff Zottys spanning twenty years: Top, 6½″/17 cm., raised script button, No. 6317,1, tag on right arm seam, "Made in US-Zone, Germany"; squeaker, ca. 1950. Bottom seated: 8½″/22 cm., incised script button, No. 0300/22; new C.T., original blue ribbon; squeaker, ca. 1970s. Standing right: 12½″/32 cm., original blue ribbon, deeper voiced squeaker. Seated in bear cart made by Rosemary Volpi: 18″/45 cm., *very* gregarious, his growler works constantly. All with shaggy frosted carmel color mohair, gold mohair chest plate; f.j., soft stuffed, sheared mohair snout with open felt mouth, air-brushed tongue, glass eyes, brown twisted floss nose/mouth, felt pads. Children and adults alike are charmed by his downward facing paws. The smallest (6½″/17 cm.) and the largest (20″/50 cm.) are hardest to find; others are abundant. Book: *Little Bear and His Friends*, Rand McNally (1933). Courtesy Nan C. Moorehead.

Grisly: Left, ca. 1970s, 21″/53 cm., beige plush, stuffed with crinkly material and cotton, f.j., light tan mohair lined ears and inset snout; floss (horizontal) nose/mouth, plastic eyes, pink felt pads, no claws; voice box. Original pink bow with two tags attached: The logo of Grisly, a needle and thread superimposed upon a standing bear; "Waschbares Grisly, Spieltier Ges. Gesch. Made in Western Germany." Right, ca. 1960s, 29″/74 cm., same as above but glass eyes. Grisly was founded in 1954 as a cottage industry. There was and still is consumer demand for the high quality Teddy Bears and animals at affordable prices. Many of these have reached the collector's market. Courtesy Stephanie Manley.

Blue Boy Bear: Teddy "Clemens," (German), 8″/20 cm., light tan mohair, straw and soft stuffed, f.j., glass eyes, black floss nose/mouth, no claws, peach velour pads; a soft look enchanced by asymmetrical ears and pudgy tummy, ca. late 1960s. Courtesy Dee Hockenberry.

"Zooby" advertised as "Zoo Bear" in 1964. The name is derived from the German *zoobaby*. This baby-like quality is well portrayed: 11″/28 cm. (one size only), No. 4328,02 retailed for $7.50 in 1964. Fur is pinkish tan mohair, shaved mohair snout; straw stuffed, swivel head, jointed arms (permanently bent at the elbow), stationary legs; glass eyes; brown twisted floss nose, open felt mouth; felt claws on shaved mohair feet with plastic soles, no paw pads. The novice collector could confuse "Zooby" with "Teddy Baby." Rare. Courtesy Dee Hockenberry.

"Character, Designed by Character Novelty Co., Inc., So. Norwalk, Conn." tag sewn into left ear seam where most "Character" tags are found. Shaggy soft synthetic plush that mats easily: 22"/56 cm., f.j., stuffed with styrofoam pellets which make him light in weight, red felt mouth and black felt nose, *glass* eyes, beige felt ear linings and pads with three painted claws, ca. 1970. (Author)

"No honey in this log!" Tan wooly plush, 15"/38 cm., unjointed, hard stuffed head, soft body, plastic eyes, glued-on brown felt nose, stitched mouth; white felt paw pads and inset snout. Tagged, "Kuddles Teddy, Knickerbocker," (Knickerbocker often placed tags in front center seam); nicely shaped body/limbs built to sit without joints, ca. 1960. In time this type of Teddy Bear will increase in value. Courtesy Kay Bransky.

Steiff bear in Easter wagon, F.A.O. Schwarz special: 8"/20 cm., brown plush, soft stuffed, jointed head, glass eyes, twisted floss nose/mouth. Steiff button in ear, original ribbon and Schwarz wooden tag. The only body shape is two small feet at bottom front; squeaker in *bottom*. An unusual example with inset snout and his own Easter wagon 8½"/22 cm. long, ca. 1960. Courtesy Nancy Crane.

Berg Bears from Austria, 1946 to present. Left, 7"/18 cm., white mohair, hard stuffed, f.j., glass eyes, black floss nose; no pads or voice box; red metal heart (trademark) attached to chest; older. Right, 5¾"/15 cm., bright gold plush of 25% wool, 75% cotton; hard stuffed, f.j., plastic eyes, black floss nose/mouth; felt pads; tag behind ear says, "Berg." Label on leg, "Made in Austria." Today the smallest size Berg bear is unjointed. Courtesy Marlene Wendt.

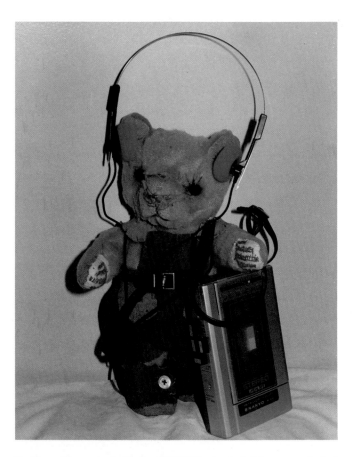

"And please Santa, bring me a Teddy Bear," says the Gebr. Hermann "Zotty" (from the German *zottig* meaning "shaggy"): 11"/28 cm., platinum frosted long pile mohair (no chest plate that the Steiff "Zotty" has); soft stuffed; f.j., glass eyes; nose is fine yarn with a *straight* stitch extending downward both sides; open felt mouth; felt pads; squeaker. Christmas stocking is counted cross stitch. Courtesy Nancy Crane.

Teddy with roots in Italy: 12½"/32 cm., bright orange faded to gold short pile mohair, straw stuffed, f.j.; eyes replaced with faceted buttons; the nose was restitched at the same time the eyelashes were applied. Purchased (1962) in Italy; owner's Italian grandmother made the alpine outfit. The beloved companion of Lisa Stanziale has travelled to Carnegie Melon Univ. and is current with a "Walkman." Worn but cute.

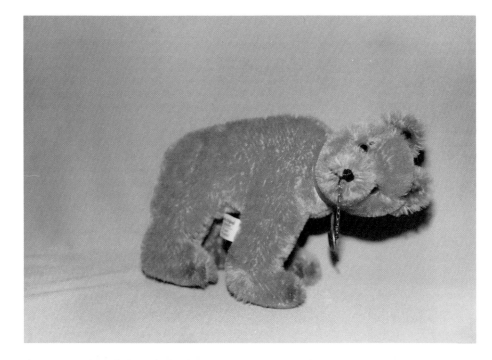

Gebr. Hermann KG, bear on all fours: 5″/12.5 cm. high, 7″/17.5 cm. long, golden tan mohair, jointed at neck (present models are unjointed), brown plastic eyes, black floss nose/mouth and claws; felt pads; original red collar with gold metal chain; tagged, ca. 1970s. Note the standing bear has the sweet face recognizable as "Hermann." Courtesy Wanda Loukides.

Gebr. Hermann KG Catalog, ca. 1970s.

Collectibles from the 1970s made for a baby: "Cosy Teddy," 7½"/20 cm., No. 4764/20, Dralon, soft stuffed, f.j., plastic eyes, floss nose, open felt mouth, felt pads; original ribbon; incised button; made in white, 1967-1974. Middle: "Lully Baby," taken from the German *einlullen* (to lull a restless infant), 8½"/22 cm., No. 7322, mohair with chest plate, soft stuffed, swivel head, glass eyes, floss nose/open mouth; working squeaker; made mid 1950s-1965 with glass eyes; 1965-1975 with plastic eyes. Right: "Cosy Orsi," 8"/20 cm., No. 4840, Dralon stuffed with foam, swivel head, floss nose/open mouth, plastic eyes, felt pads. Made with slight variations, 1950s-1978. Courtesy Kirk Stines.

Elvis Presley Teddy Bear: 10"/25 cm., black synthetic plush, soft stuffed, unjointed, glassene eyes; original Elvis pin, "Elvis Summer Festival, Sahara, Tahoe, R.C.A. Records." Given by Elvis to employees and a chosen few, ca. early 1970s. Paper of authenticity available. Bear is tagged, "Coronet Toy Manufacturer, Seattle, Wash." Courtesy Kay Bransky.

"Minky Zotty," 11"/28 cm., No. 0302/28 (made also in 14"/35 cm. size and a platinum color, 1970-1977); mink imitation, 80% Dralon, 20% cotton; shaved tan mohair inset snout; twisted floss nose; orange felt open mouth to match the pads. Note the short legs, downward paws, *white* chest plate to dramatize the unusual oriental features. Since "Minky" was produced during the transition in paper chest tags, he can be found with either the old bear tag or the new circle. Most collectors prefer the old tags. It is a form of upgrading. Courtesy Rosemary Moran.

Animal Fair's exceptionally well designed posable bean bag-type animals: 9″/23 cm., synthetic fleece covering, foam stuffed head, plastic pellets stuff body/limbs; unjointed; hard plastic eyes, felt nose. Teddy Bear, (1974); the well-known dog, "Henry," (1971); Panda, (1974). A young child's hand-washable toy with potential collectibility. (Author).

"Banker Bear" tagged "Animal Toys Plus, Inc. 1979": 16″/41 cm., brown plush, soft stuffed, unjointed, plastic eyes, glued-on black felt nose/mouth and red tongue. Original removable blue felt jacket/vest; made-to-body spats. Fine quality dressed Teddy. Courtesy Bill Gardner.

"Eden Toys, Inc. N.Y."; 14″/36 cm., sitting bear, thick gold plush, nylon fiber stuffed, unjointed, plastic eye, floss nose/red felt mouth, velveteen pads. Note the pudgy baby body with nicely curved arms and legs and the *triangular* shape of head, ca. 1975. Courtesy Bill Gardner.

"And the lamb and the bear will lie down together": 25"/64 cm. giant, gold dyed lambskin, bright blue plastic eyes, open red felt mouth, f.j.; tagged, "Pleiade, Sao Paulo Ind., Brasil EIRA." Rather than import costly mohair, Brazil uses native materials such as lamb's wool, ca. 1970. Courtesy Roberta Viscusi.

"Teddy Bear": 16"/41 cm., brown plush, beige plush pads and ear linings; soft stuffed; unjointed; vinyl-like molded head/painted features; original red ribbon; removable paper "belt"; cloth tag on left leg, "Copyright 1980 - teddy bear, Made by Calif. Stuffed Toys - Wes Soderstrom." Wonderful caricature; this type soon vaporizes from the market place. Courtesy Wanda Loukides.

Contemporary Teddy Bears

Misha, 1980 Olympic mascot: 12″/30 cm., seldom seen original Dakin issue with made-to-body suit. The Olmpic belt is *printed* on. A collector must be prepared to pay a premium for a rare example of a common toy.

Secure resale value: 1982 "Teddy Bear Tea Party"; Limited Edition (10,000) to celebrate the first birthday of the Baby Bear from the 1981 Limited Edition Mother/Baby. White, brown, honey and caramel mohair, f.j. Teddies, 7″/18 cm.; voice box. A 15-piece porcelain tea set with the Steiff logo accompanies them; *must* be mint in the diarama box. Issue price, $175.00. (Author).

Late in 1983 "Klein Archie" (Little Archie) came from Germany to the Enchanted Doll House in celebration of their twentieth birthday. He is a diminutive version of their 6'/183 cm. Steiff bear named "Archie," the Official Greeter since 1971. "Klein Archie" was made in a Limited Edition of 2,500 worldwide, and together with the 1983 Richard Steiff grey bear is Steiff's most noteworthy limited issue of that year. Steiff bears in an unjointed, upright stance are collectible; few were made, for example: "Bear Cub," 31½"/80 cm., ca. 1973. "Klein Archie," 16"/40 cm., has especially thick brown mohair, inset beige mohair snout, plastic eyes, leatherette nose, leatherette foot pads on substantial feet for standing anywhere, light orange felt paw pads; the 4 double weight felt claws complete his "cub in the woods" look; vocal growler; well set ears with large gold incised Steiff button; yellow cloth I.D. tag No. 0140/38. His low shouldered stance gives him great "presence." Increasing in value, yet affordable. (Author).

Gebr. Hermann KG, "Seebar": 11"/28 cm., gold synthetic plush, sewn-to-body pants and sailor's cap; embedded plastic pipe. Marketed a short time, ca. 1984. In the future when contemporary bears become antiques, it will be important to have the manufacturer documented. Courtesy Rosemary Moran.

Left: 1983, first year of Merrythought's Limited Edition (2,500) "Edwardian," 15″/38 cm., advertised as "matted" old gold mohair, straw stuffed head, firmly cotton stuffed body/limbs, f.j., snout clipped to plastic eyes, brown wool yarn nose/mouth, tan felt pads with the distinctive Merrythought feature of embroidered claws on the face of paw pads; growler. Machine-stitched Merrythought tag on right foot pad as well as I.D. tag sewn into left side seam. 1984 Limited Edition (2,500) "Long Snout," 16″/41 cm., thick light gold mohair, straw and cotton stuffed, f.j., plastic eyes, black stitched nose/mouth, no claws, white felt pads; growler. Note arms are "straight out" with curved paws; longish feet. There are 3 tags to prove I.D. Scarf added. This high quality bear has a special look and is already increasing in value. The 1984 retail, $83.00. (Author)

Steiff's jointed Pandas were on the market only 1984-1985: 11½″/29 cm. and 13½″/35 cm., a replica from 1938, mohair, f.j., with same self-standing feet, grey felt pads; squeeze voice box. There were not good sellers. At a distance there was not enough difference between them and Pandas of other manufacturers. Issue price, $85.00 and $110.00. Courtesy Rosemary Moran.

Grisly bear: 9″/23 cm., red mohair; unknown stuffing; f.j., plastic eyes, floss nose; white mohair pads and inset snout; blue tag on arm reads "465/20." Note the large head on broad shoulders with a slim body and straight slim limbs. Grisly used kelly green mohair on some models. These bright colors were made for the American market, ca. 1980. Courtesy Lisa Osta.

"Big Bear," 63"/160 cm., celebrated the Detroit Tigers' 1984 victories and has never given up hope. The Tom Sellick of "Bearsville." Steiff STUDIO lying polar bear, woven fur/mohair, No. 0472/99. Designed as decorative accents for *studio* decor, they are called STUDIO which implies life-size. Courtesy Nancy Crane.

Bremen Black Bear made entirely in the U.S.A.: 16"/40.5 cm., highest quality mink-like plush with guard hairs, f.j., inset sheared plush snout and pads, plastic eyes and composition nose; dated with a tag sewn into left arm seam; a cardboard I.D. tag is attached to the red leather collar. Limited to 200 pieces in 1985, he is made exclusively for The Bremen Bear Co. Ltd. by Sheram Puppets, Inc., Columbus, Ohio. There are 14 bears in this outstanding line ranging from 15"/38 cm. to 33"/84 cm.; all are beautifully proportioned animals that will last for generations. Issued in 1985 at $40.00. (Author).

1984 Goldilocks and the Three Bears, by Suzanne Gibson and Steiff: Papa, 13"/32 cm. No. 0173/32; Mama, 12"/30 cm.; Baby, 10"/25 cm.; Goldilocks, 16"/40.5 cm. She is designed by the outstanding doll artist, Suzanne Gibson, who also designed the clothes for the bear family. The Teddy Bears have brown glass eyes, brown twisted floss nose/mouth, 4 claws, curved paws and long feet with felt pads. Note the center seam in head makes a broad snout. Each bear has a white cloth I.D. tag. This set was limited to 2,000 and distributed by Reeves International, Inc., New York. The doll was manufactured and assembled in the USA; the clothing made in Taiwan. Due to demand for the large set (shown), in 1985 Goldilocks became 8"/20 cm. with bears to scale; still the same outfits. This set is limited to 5,000 worldwide. The investment potential is greater for the *first*, more limited, set. In 1984 it retailed for $300.00. Courtesy Edward Moriuchi.

Artist Teddy Bears

A special tribute must be paid to Beverly Port, founder of the "American Teddy Bear Artist" movement. For the past 25 years, this pioneer has written about, repaired as well as made, and collected Teddy Bears. Beverly has been the inspiration and role model for thousands of artists and promoted the Teddy Bear as an art form. She has defined terms. For example: the Cottage Industry Artist Bear; the Artist Original Bear (creating the first design); "handmade" where many can be manufactured (the long seams are machine stitched); "handstitched" where there is no machine stitching, etc. Her magical and whimsical designs have touched a nostalgic chord in the hearts of people around the world. She is internationally acclaimed for her excellence in design, craftsmanship and originality. The above special exhibit (1984) shows some of Beverly Port's original and copyrighted (1960-1980) designs ranging from 5″/13 cm. to 36″/91 cm. tall. As the leader in her field, she has designed well over 150 different bears, all with captivating names such as: Toybox Teddy; Heinrich Bearkin; Nursemaid and Baby Brat; Little Boy Bear; Raggedy Bear; Threadbear and Hollybeary; Jingles; Emily Bearkin and her husband Bearon Beowolf Bearkin; Tedwina, etc. The Artist Bear movement is growing by leaps and bounds and is a purely American phenomena that is already spreading to Europe. This trendsetting artist has branched out into other animals including bunnies. Courtesy Beverly Port.

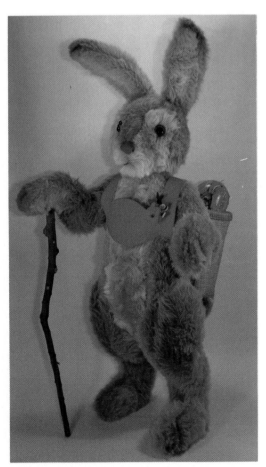

His official name is "Easter Bunny"; also known as "E.B."; 36″/91 cm.; European curly acrylic that is two-tone; polyester stuffed; jointed arms and legs, swivel head; apparatus in body moves head when the tail is turned; music box plays "Easter Parade"; leather harness decorated with handmade felt flowers. Designed and meticulously made by Beverly Port, "E.B." captures the classic Easter memories of childhood. One of a kind.

"Mr. Cinnamon Bear," from the 1907 book of that name: 18"/46 cm., cinnamon mohair head and hands, canvas body f.j., straw and cotton stuffed, glass eyes, black stitched nose/mouth, felt hand pads; wearing a removable brown wool suit that is lined, cotton shirt and oversize rayon bowtie, ultra suede shoes; stamped at back neck onto fabric body, "A Bear by Nett." Many people are partial to clothed bears. A *very* limited edition in 1985. Few Teddy Bears are worthy of a setting as grand as the Mount St. Helen's Doll House by Noel and Pat Thomas, Gardner collection.

"Angel Moran," 16"/40.5 cm., designed by Linda Spiegel of Bearly There Co.; made in a Limited Edition of 6 expressly for My Favorite Dolls Shop to honor Rosemary Moran's daughter, Angel. A magenta colored 1930s tapestry weave upholstery fabric was chosen for the bear covering. The small numbers in which Artist's Bears are made compared to the huge quantities of industrially manufactured bears, as well as the vastly different marketing procedures, make them a stimulating choice for a collection.

Mink Teddy Bear created by Chris McWilliams: 8"/20 cm., recycled mink, polyfill stuffed, f.j. by plastic doll joints, glass eyes, floss nose, ultra suede pads and bowtie. Note the elegant mink with beautiful highlighting that cannot be captured by synthetic fur; entirely hand stitched.

"Fritz" is the largest bear in Maria Schmidt's *Charlestowne Bear* line: 33″/84 cm., long (1″/2.5 cm.) honey colored mohair, f.j., solid black glass eyes, clipped snout, black floss nose/mouth and claws, double padded tan felt pads, elongated features, hump; leather collar with bells. Note the center seam in head gusset giving him a charming antique look. "Fritz" is a work of soft sculpture, one of the rare forms of art that you not only love, but that you can hug. Courtesy Maria Schmidt.

"Boscoe," 23″/58.5 cm., long pile (1″/2.5 cm.) off-white imported mohair styled after a 1920s German-type Teddy Bear; firmly fiberfill stuffed, f.j., enameled brown glass eyes; rust floss vertical nose/mouth, 4 claws; smiling face with clipped snout; large hump, long curved arms, big feet with camel wool pads; limited edition of 500. This lovable bear was created in 1985 by Maria Schmidt and has already shown investment potential.

Maria Schmidt is a free lance artist who began making Teddy Bears in 1983. Unable to find a long armed, humped back Teddy to buy, she adhered to the adage: "If you can't find it, make it yourself." Maria's work is greatly influenced by fine early German bears. The quality and character of her work reaches toward perfection of form and makes for countless hours of tedious minor pattern changes. A new bear will start as a figure in her imagination that insists on being created. Usually she will think about it for weeks before starting a pattern. Maria develops a total *mental* image of the bear, viewing him from all angles. Slowly the desired shape emerges and after many prototypes a "final" bear pattern will be ready for production. (The two prototypes for "Boscoe" were made from an old white cashmere coat.) Her bears are not accidents; they are extremely well thought out and researched pieces. It is a huge task to complete a pattern and construct the bear that is in her mind. A bear will take any where from several days to several weeks before she is completely satisfied with him. Though each bear remains an individual, she tries to impart as close a resemblance to one another as possible; keeping true both type and character. Her bears are in limited supply as all work is executed solely by the artist.

"Spike," light hearted and trendy, handmade by Debra Demosthenes: 14″/36 cm. and 16″/41 cm., acrylic fur, f.j., humpbacked bear with washer locked eyes; fine construction in this take-off of the English punk kid. Note the hand colored mohawks with accent colors, the felt spiked collar and safety pin earring. Courtesy Rosemary Moran.

Antique Teddy Bear collectors avidly collect artist bears such as those designed and handmade by Diane Gard. The choice of fabric for the Teddy Bear is of premier importance. The use of old and unusual fur fabrics has become Diane's trademark. "Rough Rider," 15″/38 cm., is fully jointed and made from an original bolt of fabric used to upholster Pierce Arrow Automobiles of the 1930s. Each bear is named for a member of the heroic Rough Rider regiment. "Liberty Bear," 14″/36 cm. is fully jointed and made from the original red mohair fabric used on the seats of the 1904 Liberty Opera House in Western Colorado. Note the traditional styling and fine workmanship.

"Yodee," 14″/36 cm., made from an old coat, f.j., soft stuffed, brown hand stitched nose/mouth, safety lock eyes of brown acrylic, growler. Exclamation Card Co. of CA is featuring him on 1987 greeting cards. Roberta Viscusi's original design that she makes to give away to sick children in need of comfort. They are child proof and will last. "Yodee" wears Cabbage Patch clothes perfectly. Great Expression.

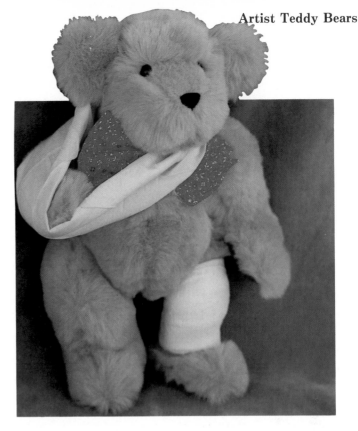

Musical bear by artist Jenny Krantz: 17″/43 cm., blonde acrylic plush, f.j.; floppy cuddly bear; felt/flannel ear linings and pads. Purchased in 1984 for $50.00. With the surge of interest in artist's bears today, the early models have shown steady appreciation. Jenny is a member of The American Teddy Bear Artist Guild. Steiff, 10″/25 cm., No. 0202/26 "Original Teddy," Trevira velvet pads, ca. 1960s. Courtesy Nancy Crane.

Bear with a special purpose created by Roberta Viscusi, Napa, CA. "Ouchy," 22″/56 cm. highest quality plush, poly-fill stuffed, f.j., safety lock eyes, stitched nose/mouth, leather pads, hump and growler. A removable cast made to surgeon's specifications is put on the exact fractured limb of person being given the artist bear. This is the blonde "Bentley" model but any of her designs can be cast.

Teddy Roosevelt artist bear tagged, "Double Patti Products, copyright 1984, Berkeley, CA": 12″/30 cm., seated, unjointed, firmly cotton stuffed, thick gray plush well-contoured from a complex pattern; face is needle sculpted from nylon hose, plastic disc eyes, brass monocle sewn on, plush fur eyebrows and moustache, wool flannel bowtie. A row of white pony beads is sewn on for teeth. Theodore Roosevelt outwardly was a loud, blustering man who was inordinately proud of his teeth. Inwardly, he was a "softy." All well portrayed by this innovative bear bought for the author by her son at the Polk St. Art Fair, San Francisco, 1985. Hermann, 8″/20 cm. (1978), f.j., gold mohair, jersey pads. Pads on Hermann bears: 1920s-1970s, felt or mohair; 1977-1979, jersey; 1980 to present, felt or mohair. He is wearing one of 20 stock shirt designs (in 8 colors) made by Shirts Illustrated.

Few Kings are made: 24″/60 cm., light tan plush head, paws and feet; red velvet body and cape with tan satin lining, black plastic eyes, black leather nose. Pads are plush. A jeweled crown is added to make him "King of the Mardi Gras." Fully jointed and well crafted by C.J. Prince, Garland, Texas (1984). Courtesy Sammie Chambliss.

VII. Wheeled Animals

Somewhat fiercely portrayed, a rare example of the bear as bruin: 8½"/22 cm. high, 12"/30.5 cm. long, mohair over papier mache; brown glass eyes; black molded nose, open mouth with molded teeth; pairs of small cast iron wheels with crossbar individually attached to paws; pull the ring *under* body and he growls to provide the nursey child with further fantasy, ca. 1900. Courtesy Dot Franklin.

Many collectors are looking for bears on wheels. As the jointed Teddy Bears get harder to find, people turn to the next closest thing (which is actually more rare). Prices on these wheeled bears (and all wheeled animals) are unsettled. Lifesize: 30"/76 cm. high, 40"/102 cm. long, thick pile cinnamon color mohair turned greyish; all straw stuffed with hardwood armature; head is jointed by large hardwood discs occupying the entire neck space; large black wooden shoe button-type eyes deeply set; life-like long, well tapered snout; black twisted hard cotton floss nose/mouth, 4 claws each with double strand of floss; beaver felt pads on large, long feet; standing on sturdy axles attached to cast iron wheels with 6 spokes; no voice box; missing the left ear where Steiff button is found. He is listing to the right, a result of being mounted from the left in the nursery ca. 1908. This toy could carry a large amount of weight and has withstood years of love and abuse in the play room. The modelling on this "art as toy" is such that every muscle and layer of fat under the fur covering can be visualized. The bandaged legs can be restored. Extremely difficult to replace this large size. (Author).

Since the 16th century, much has been written about the popularity of animal pull/riding toys. This early 20th cent. example exhibits all the sculptural beauty and strength of the bear in nature. Steiff printed button "ff" underscored: 17"/43 cm. high, 24"/61 cm., golden brown mohair, straw stuffed, unjointed; black shoe button eyes; black twisted hard cotton floss nose/mouth, 4 claws; felt pads on long feet; deep sound to pull ring voice box; hump; tail. He stands firmly on the axles attached to cast iron wheels with 6 spokes. It is the wise collector who stalks these rare specimans with I.D. Courtesy Dee Hockenberry.

Pull toy for a child; riding toy for an antique doll: 11"/28 cm. high, 12"/30.5 cm. long, grey mohair, felt tusks; eyes once had painted backs but are clear now; original circus blanket with embroidered scroll in the figure "28" (the size in cm.); note the 4 spoked cast iron wheels and no crossbar (typical of the smaller toys). 1925 appears to be the last year Steiff used cast iron wheels. Courtesy Tom and Susie Stroud.

Goats rather than ponies were fashionable in the 17th century. During the 19th century, they again came into vogue: 13"/33 cm. high, 12"/30.5 cm. long, goat fur over papier mache body, glass eyes, molded nose; metal wheels. When the head is pulled back, he bleats. Courtesy Dot Franklin.

Riding high: Top Teddy Bear, 15″/38 cm., dark grey (desirable color) long pile mohair, firmly stuffed with kapok, disc jointed head and arms, unjointed floppy legs (unique combination of jointing); amber glass eyes, black floss nose/mouth and claws, *no* pads, squeaker stamped "Germany;" small ears hidden in fur, wide head, short arms, ca. 1930. Add value for his determined expression. Bear on Wheels: 13½″/34 cm. high, 21″/53 cm. long, grey mohair, hard stuffed straw, unjointed, shoe button eyes, black floss nose/mouth, felt pads; steel wheel base with hard rubber tires on disc wheels, ca. 1920. The uncommon grey of both bears adds value. Courtesy Marlene Wendt.

"Record Teddy" (scooter cart): 10″/25 cm., gold mohair, straw stuffed, f.j., black shoe button eyes, tan felt paw pads (repaired); the Teddy is "made-on" cart that has a metal frame with wooden wheels marked, "Steiff"; he pumps up and down when the toy is pulled along. Rare. Courtesy Helen Sieverling.

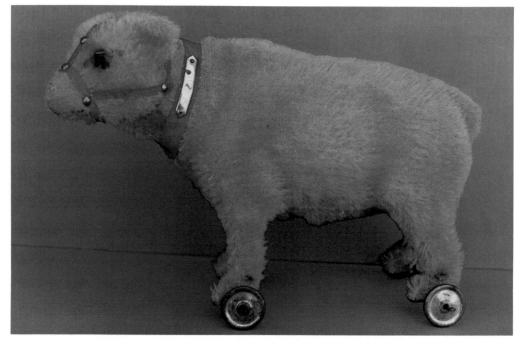

Japan or German: 7″/18 cm. high, 10″/25 cm. long, short sparse gold mohair over papier mache, glass "stalk" eyes, molded ears and tail, oil cloth-type pads, muzzle and collar (tacked on); hole in chest where pull chain once was. All on pot metal wheels; unusually fine condition for this lesser quality toy, ca. 1920s. At a reasonable price, the example rounds out a collection of wheeled bears.

Hand wagon, 25″/64 cm. long, natural varnished wood, disc wheels/black rubber tires; packs by dismounting axles. In this vein, Steiff also made a wheel barrow, farm cart, carts with wooden horse, travelling cage, various play cars and trucks, scooters, pedal cars, coasters, etc. "Jocko," 19½″/50 cm., No. 0020/50, fur imitation, dangling limbs, soft stuffed, plastic eyes, trevira velvet face, hands and ears; airbrushed markings. Retailed for $57.00 in 1975. Courtesy Claudia Shotwell.

Riding horse: 23″/58 cm. high, rust and white mohair, straw stuffed, glass eyes, white horsehair mane and tail, original well made saddle; all mounted on metal wheels/black rubber tires, ca. 1940. The saddle (Steiff used only red leather during this period), conformation of the head and the wheel base show that it is not Steiff. There are many collectors of monkeys because of the great variety available. Left: Steiff "Mungo," 6½″/17 cm., seen elsewhere. Center: 19″/48 cm. chimp, long shaggy gold mohair tipped with brown, white beard, felt face, ears and paws, glass eyes, wire armature in limbs, jointed head, unknown maker, ca. 1960. Right: 11″/28 cm., tagged "Rushton." Bellhop monkey, brown cotton plush, vinyl mask face, big ears, felt paws, wire armature in limbs and tail, ca. 1950. All courtesy Nan C. Moorehead.

Chocolate brown rayon velour: 13″/33 cm. high, 24″/61 cm. long, straw stuffed, unjointed, *celluloid* eyes, ears set well forward. Note the extra long neck and pronounced hump. Red wooden wheels on wood frame with feet secured to *crossbar*; whereas Steiff positions one or both back feet *on* the rear axle. Maker unknown, ca. 1940. Some wear. Courtesy Diane Hoffman.

Simmental steer (European breed): 9½″/24 cm. high, 13″/33 cm. long, printed Steiff button "ff" underscored, traces of white I.D. tag (1905-1926): inset brown and white mohair; straw stuffed; unjointed; black shoe button eyes backed with white felt to give dimension for a limpid-eye look; straw stuffed felt horns/wire armature; missing tail; one cast iron wheel is replaced. In 1925 this farm animal is seen on both cast iron and wooden wheels. Some pull toys from this early period are worth 100% more. They include: pigs, geese, swans, buffalo and giraffes. Reasonable condition, ca. 1913. Courtesy Dee Hockenberry.

A Christmas toy for Eloise Wilkin's 25″/64 cm. "Baby Dear One," a bouncy one-year old with two front teeth (1962): Terrier, 11″/28 cm. high, 13″/33 cm. long, all straw stuffed, unjointed, light brown markings on white mohair, brown glass eyes, black floss nose, 2 floss claws; sewn down ears. Note the plastic coated collar with a blank silver oval medallion. The dog is attached to the gold painted metal frame by heavy floss; European manufacture, ca. 1950. (Author).

Two fine examples of the lure of the moving toy for the young child, ca. 1920-1930. Cat, 10″/25 cm. long, 7″/17.5 cm. high, straw stuffed, jointed head, glass eyes, pink embroidered nose/mouth, short prickly mohair; mounted on axle. The metal wheels are embossed "ANIMOBILE ANIMATE TOY" on 3 wheels; one rear wheel reads "SAVAGE PATENTS J.S. & FOREIGN PATS. PENDING." Jointed dog: 10″/25 cm. long, straw stuffed, f.j., mohair, glass eyes, detailed nose/mouth; wheels on feet. Maker unknown. Courtesy Kay Bransky.

Riding tiger: 20″/50 cm. tall, No. 70/1350,2, airbrushed mohair in tigered stripes; green glass eyes, open felt mouth with plastic teeth; steel frame; disc/rubber wheels; pull growler. In addition to bears and elephants, Steiff made a variety of riding animals: Poodle, St. Bernard, Foxterrier, ladybug, donkey, Boxer, Scotty, Sealyham (white Scotty), Police Dog, camel, seal, goldfish, lion, zebra, ox, lamb and Airedale. All but the pony, donkey and elephant are considered hard to find, ca. late 1950s.

Sunny Meadow, good companions: "S.A.F." (Austria), black and gold tag in left ear (embroidered Teddy on reverse), 23″/58.5 cm., bright gold mohair, straw stuffed, f.j., hard plastic eyes, black floss nose/mouth and claws, felt pads; growler. High quality European import, ca. 1960. Original tag adds value. Bear on wheels, 19″/48 cm. high, 26″/66 cm. long, brown mohair, sheared beige mohair inset snout straw stuffed, unjointed, glass eyes, black twisted floss nose/mouth, heavy beige floss claws, felt pads/cardboard innersoles; metal rod in feet attaches bear to the steel frame with disc wheels and white rubber tires; pull ring voice. Old leather replaces the ears. They were used as handlebars on these toys, making them vulnerable. Tag, "Made in U.S. Zone Germany" on inseam of leg ca. 1950. Courtesy Marlene Wendt.

Riding pony: 31½″/80 cm. tall, No. 1380,2, brown mohair/airbrushed markings, straw stuffed, steel frame, glass eyes, felt pads, pull voice box, disc wheels/white rubber tires; detachable wooden rocker. Comparing to today's squared-off look, note the life-like sculpturing and slender conformation of this earlier model purchased in West Berlin, ca. late 1950s-1960. Wooden rockers were sold separately as an accessory for riding animals. Courtesy Claudia Shotwell.

Mechanical Animals

Mechanical candy container rabbit: 8"/20 cm., natural fur covering over cardboard; the candy tube opens at bottom. There is a metal rod attached to tail; when leveraged, the ears and hands move and he squeaks. Unique and extremely rare, ca. early 1900s. Courtesy Tom and Susie Stroud.

Possum as a trapeze toy, 6"/15 cm., grey and white rabbit fur over cardboard armature body, jointed by wires, *celluloid* button eyes. Rare example of a hand toy during the Billy Possum era, ca. 1910. Mint. (Author).

Mechanical Polar Bears are unusual: 9"/23 cm. high, 16½"/42 cm. long, white fur covers metal and papier mache frame; before the widespread use of mohair, mechanicals often had animal skin coverings; clear glass eyes with black pupil, molded black nose, black wood feet. When the key is wound, he walks forward moving head from side to side. These delicate mechanisms did not withstand play. Probable French, ca. 1900. Turn-of-the century mechanicals are seldom found for sale or in collections today. Courtesy Dot Franklin.

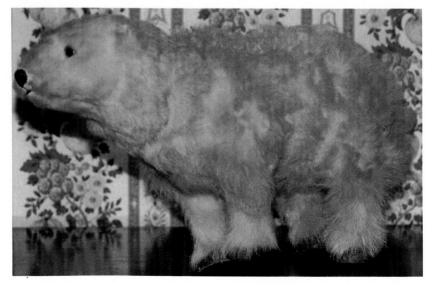

Steiff tumbler: 13″/33 cm., light golden plush on a dark woven backing called "two-tone" mohair; straw stuffed, f.j., shoe button eyes; horizontal floss nose; felt pads. The clockwork mechanism inside the body is connected to the arms which go around when wound up. It was advertised that this mechanism would not be damaged by turning the wrong way. There was a somersaulting chimpanzee made at the same time, ca. 1911-1913. Old printed button "ff" underscored. Rare. Courtesy Beverly Port.

Key wind walking/nodding bear: 8″/20 cm. long, tipped beige mohair, straw stuffed head, metal body, shoe button eyes, floss nose/mouth. Purchased at 1939 New York World's Fair. Great face. Possible Schuco. Courtesy Ellyn McCorkell.

Electrified twist 'n turn bear: 24″/61 cm., composition-type frame covered with orange early synthetic plush. Motor causes bear to twist from side to side while the head moves; kept in storage until Christmas when it delights young and old alike. Store display piece, ca. 1930. Courtesy Diane Hoffman.

Animated dog: 6½"/16.5 cm. long, black cotton plush, white cotton plush chest plate, celluloid eyes, tin nose (suggests 1930s). Key wind; walks on the jointed metal legs while head moves. Original orange rayon ribbon and paper bucket. Courtesy Gaye N. Delling.

Mechanical Irish Terrier: 11"/28 cm., high, 12"/30 cm. long, thick pile white mohair with airbrushed markings, jointed head, brown mohair ears, felt nose, glass eyes, original red leatherette collar; two knobs at rear of head open mouth to "bark." An unusual example of an animated toy, ca. 1950, tagged, "Made in Republic of Ireland." Courtesy Nan C. Moorehead.

Tumbling Bear: 13"/33 cm., motion activated by winding the long stiff arms; reddish brown coton/rayon plush, beige plush snout, ear linings, paws and pads; stitched jointed short legs; cotton stuffed body, amber glass eyes, red felt tongue, molded nose, original green felt vest; American, ca. 1940s. "Now look here, Bear," the Terrier seems to say: 7"/18 cm. high, 9½"/24 cm. long, brown and black spotted mohair, straw stuffed, glass eyes, black *leather* nose, felt mouth, thread claws, velvet pads. Maker unknown, ca. 1950-1960. Courtesy Peggy Young.

Drinking Bear, battery-operated toy made in Japan, ca. 1950: 9½"/24 cm., synthetic plush on tin, plastic snout, glass eyes, ears sliced in. Before the advent of the computer chip, Japan used their skills to create often complex movements in bear toys. The classic drinking motion (most often found) is a copy of an earlier foreign design with a key-wind mechanism. Many of today's collectors are of the age to have played with these and are anxious to recover their toys. A good speculation, MIB. Courtesy Diane Hoffman.

Mechanical showpiece, ca. 1980: Depicts Steiff animals and "Mecki Characters" performing tasks in a variety of movements. The first Steiff animated display was created in 1912. Courtesy Hobby Center Toys.

Steiff continues to make animated displays for special exhibits and some toy stores. The animals are wearing "hard hats" in these segments of the construction scene, ca. 1980. Courtesy Hobby Center Toys on loan from Reeves International, Inc.

Steiff Special Exhibit

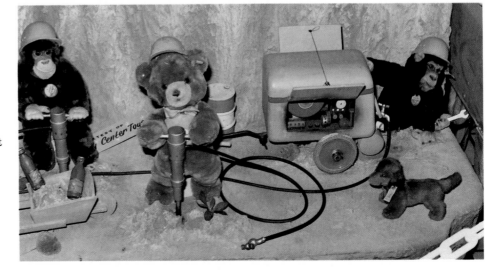

Steiff special exhibit

VIII. Schuco Teddy Bears and Animals

Emerald green compact bear: 3½″/9 cm., ca. 1920-1930, mohair over a metal frame, wire jointed arms and legs, swivel head, black metal eyes, black floss nose/mouth; removing the head reveals an oval mirror, powder puff and tray. Rare color; the compact bear is harder to find than the perfume bottle bear. There exists an ingenious compact bear with the addition of lipstick in the head. Center: 4½″/12 cm., ca. 1950, bright gold mohair, hard stuffed straw, wire jointed, amber glass eyes, floss nose/mouth, original ribbon; popular small size; maker unknown. Right: 4½″/11.5 cm., ca. 1920-1930, blonde mohair on metal frame, wire jointed, black metal eyes, brown thread nose/mouth. Lift off head to find the perfume bottle. Rare and desirable; every collector wants an example. Courtesy Marlene Wendt.

The earliest Schuco miniatures had tiny attached one-piece beige felt paws and feet. Since these were found to be easily removed by young fingers, they were discontinued after 1930. Monkey, 3½″/9 cm., green mohair over the patented metal form; lift head to find glass perfume bottle with stopper and long stem; swivel head, wire jointed limbs. Also made in scarlet mohair. Teddy Bear, 2½″/6 cm., bright gold mohair over metal form, fully wire jointed, black metal eyes, black thread nose/mouth. Both are rare "finds." Courtesy Maria Schmidt.

Schuco perfume bottle bear: 3¼″/9 cm., ca. 1920s, pink (rare color) mohair over the patented *metal* body, f.j.; removable head exposes thin glass bottle with original cork stopper; black metal eyes, black floss nose/mouth (4 threads on top, one lower thread from which the mouth is formed). The ear is attached with metal prongs into a depression in the head. She has always been sitting in her ca. 1920s Kilgore high chair, 3½″/9 cm., yellow painted iron with bunny rabbit filigree. The chair is padded with pink cotton sewn in a child's wide, misplaced stitches. Lesson: When you see an older Schuco, try to remove the head. Here we have two things: the essence of childhood (the toy left undisturbed in its original setting) and a rare example of the perfume bottle bear that was made in two sizes: 3½″/9 cm. and 5″/13 cm. (the latter is the more common). (Author).

Yes/No mechanism is *rare* in birds: 7"/18 cm., soft stuffed body, hard head; white mohair/airbrushed markings; glass eyes; red felt straw stuffed beak; tan felt feet; squeaker. Tail activates head movement. Missing are red and black felt scarfs tied together to look *chic*. Note the similarity of beak to Steiff's penguins. Schuco Yes/No ducks were also made, ca. 1926. Courtesy Dee Hockenberry.

Schuco treasure: 10"/25 cm. tall, gold mohair over metal torso and legs; straw stuffed head and arms; jointed arms, stationary head; glass eyes (eyes came interchangeably as glass or shoe button); black stitched nose/mouth; red felt coat and contrasting cap; black metal shoes have small wheels on soles enambling the Bellhop Bear to walk forward when key is wound, ca. 1920. Full value can be given to any mechanical toy *only* when it is operational as here. Courtesy Dot Franklin.

Schuco's wise looking cat with attached metal spectacles. 7"/18 cm., long pile snow white mohair, f.j., straw stuffed, Yes/No mechanism in tail. Fascinating *green* faceted jewel eyes that were avaialbe from the Schuco factory by special order only; pink floss nose/mouth. Also made in grey and black mohair, ca. 1924. Courtesy Tom and Susie Stroud.

Yes/No with metal spectacles securely attached into the side of head, 5"/13 cm., gold mohair, hard body, f.j., black metal eyes, black floss nose/mouth, no pads, ca. 1926. Mint. Souvenir bear, (Japan), 3¼"/8 cm., gold sparse mohair, hard stuffed straw, wire jointed, amber glass eyes, painted nose, no pads; original ribbon. Unusual feature is the attached glass bottle of scotch; tagged "Bears for Booze in Fort William Canada." Sales price 25¢, ca. 1930. Courtesy Marlene Wendt.

Schuco Teddy Bears have an appeal beyond their mechanism. Rare size, 5"/13 cm., Yes/No, gold mohair over metal form, f.j., brown glass eyes, black floss nose/mouth; wire extension on bottom operates head movement. Made in the same size, there is a later Yes/No bear with a red felt tongue, ca. 1950s (the era of red felt tongues). A premium must be added for miniaturization. Excellent condition, ca. 1920. Courtesy Wanda Loukides.

The curve of a snout, the lift of a head on these Schuco Yes/No bears manages to convey expression beyond straw and mohair. Rocking chair Teddy, 13"/33 cm., tan mohair, c. 1950. Standing, 15"/38 cm., light tan mohair head and limbs; the fabric body was dressed originally in a checked shirt and felt pants, ca. 1960. Both bears have glass eyes, floss nose/mouth and claws; felt foot pads with hardboard innersoles (for standing); downward facing paws; mechanism in tails to move heads. Courtesy Nan C. Moorehead.

"Lift Boy," also called Yes/No "Bellhop Monkey," 12″/30 cm., sewn to body felt outfit, f.j., straw stuffed, *clear* glass eyes, painted features on felt face; felt ears, brown mohair head, tail, feet and paws (shiny woven pads); working squeaker. Tail as lever operates Yes/No mechanism. Mint, ca. 1920s. Courtesy Maria Schmidt.

Yes/No mechanism exposed: Monkey head, 3½″/9 cm., works on basis of a cam. The head sits in a perforated metal dish and moves up and down by means of a cam accuated by a shaft connected to the tail. The head moves side to side by twisting the tail which turns the shaft. The metal cup at base of head provides reinforcement for the head and the anchor for cam to travel in. Arm and leg joints: The metal on cardboard disc provides a bearing surface and prevents the pin from pulling through the cardboard. Barring a natural disaster, these Yes/No toys will last for generations of play. Courtesy Connie Hart.

A gem: 14″/36 cm., gold mohair, straw stuffed rock-hard, *clear* glass eyes (typifies Schuco), vertical stitched nose with long stitches (contoured inward) on each side, 3 claws, *mohair* pads on big feet with hardboard soles for self-standing. Several types of Schuco bears had innersoles, especially the Yes/No Teddy Bear. Note the large ears that are straw stuffed and seen on some Schuco models. Identification by a former Schuco employee; ca. 1930s. Mint. Courtesy Maria Schmidt.

Blonde, long pile mohair tipped with brown, 10″/25 cm., straw hard stuffed, glass eyes, black floss nose in "life-like style"; mohair inset snout, long and sharply pointed; mohair pads (hardboard innersoles) with 3 floss claws. Hermann also used 3 claws but not the hard innersoles under their mohair pads. Purchased in Germany. Thought to be Schuco, ca. 1930. Wind-up frog, 3″/7.5 cm., airbrushed grey-green velvet, painted yellow steel frame, clear glass eyes, metal legs attached to wheels. "Schuco" original key. The highly realistic way the frog jumps forward is due to clever engineering. Some wear, ca. 1940. Courtesy Karen Frasco.

Toy bunny in Easter colors: 6″/15 cm., white cotton plush over papier mache body, pink cardboard-lined ears; glass eyes; *painted* nose/mouth; felt clothes, blue foil-covered attached hat; Schuco keywind mechanism. Rare in mint condition, ca. 1930s. Courtesy Connie Hart.

The familiar face of "Tricky," ca. 1950s to 1960s: 13″/33 cm., light gold mohair, straw stuffed, f.j., clear glass eyes, floss nose and mouth giving the perky expression; peach felt pads; non-working squeaker; posed with miniature Teddies. The tail lever is missing the mohair covering; he is hesitant about nodding. In the 1950s Steiff also made a nodding bear; the head is NOT swiveled. The most noticeable feature is that the head is attached to the torso by a *loose skin of mohair*. A rod comes through the body into the head where it is attached by a series of fittings causing the bear's head to move around and around when the tail is turned. Courtesy Kirk Stines.

Popular Dare Wright books, 9½"/24 cm. x 12¾"/32.4 cm. hardbound: Top, *The Lonely Doll*, copyright 1957, published by Doubleday & Co., NY. In 1958 Madame Alexander adapted her "Edith the Lonely Doll" from this photographic story of another doll and her two bear friends: a large Yes/No Schuco and a small Steiff "Jackie." This book was reprinted in 1984-1985 and is the easiest book of the (old) series to find. Bottom: Featured are Edith and Big Bad Bill joined by Mr. Bear and his cousins—Charles and Albert (all Schucos). Steiff's "Jackie" is again Little Bear. Copyright 1968; published by Random House, New York. Hard to find. (Author).

Appropriately named "Tricky": Yes/No cat, 8"/20 cm., off-white mohair, straw stuffed, f.j., pink floss nose/mouth, green glass eyes, black mohair ears lined with grey velveteen, peach felt pads/cardboard innersoles for standing, whiskers. Tail operates mechanism. Note the rayon bow *sewn* to chest as is typical of Schuco. Tagged "US-Zone Germany," (1945-1952). A "Tricky" cat, rabbit or dog is more rare than a Teddy Bear or monkey, yet bears command the highest prices and will continue to do so. Currently underpriced, there is greatest investment potential in the Schuco toys. (Author).

Schuco Yes/No, ca. 1950, as found photographed in Dare Wright's Lonely Doll books; 20"/51 cm. (large size).

Schuco "Goofy," 14"/36 cm., mohair head, arms and feet; red/white cotton body; jointed by bendable wire; black plastic eyes; open felt mouth and tongue (missing felt teeth); black felt nose (stuffed) and long ears; partially dressed in removable orange felt jacket. His biggest problem is his teeth as Disney collectors require Goofy to have teeth, ca. 1960. Courtesy Claudia Shotwell.

Yes/No cat with silly face: 14"/36 cm., dark brown short pile mohair, inset beige mohair face, green celluloid-type eyes, pink twisted floss nose, black floss mouth, velveteen lined ears; long pile beige mohair flounce as hands and feet (typical of Schuco); jointed by bendable wire. This same wire served for the Yes/No function: Move the long tail to manipulate head; cheaper construction, the wire often became disengaged. The removable green cotton pants and yellow felt shirt are often missing; the red/white stripe cotton blouse is sewn-to-body. He is associated with the name "Bigo Belo" and was also made in 12"/30.5 cm. size. Additionally, Schuco made a cat on all fours with this unmistakable character face, ca. 1950-1960. Surprisingly little demand. Courtesy Claudia Shotwell.

Schuco, 4½"/11 cm., key wind bought new in Germany in 1955 for $1.00. When wound he goes around in a circle beating drum; red cotton chenille hair. One of a series that includes: monkey/violin, clown/violin and monkey/drum. MIB. Courtesy Bill Gardner.

Alfred the Little Bear books displayed with Schucos. Author: Bill Binzen; published by Doubleday and Co., 1970-1974-1976. The three books have stories about Alfred the Little Bear, portrayed by a miniature Schuco. Real photographs are used to illustrate the delightful story. These books are out of print and hard to find. Courtesy Wanda Loukides.

Schuco, ca. 1963-1965: Walt Disney's *Mickey and Minnie Mouse*: 3½"/9 cm., black mohair covered pipe stem legs, arms and tail; head and body are hard; plastic nose on painted/molded tin face, black felt ears, white felt hands, yellow plastic shoes, red felt clothes with white rayon trim. Purchased in 1963 for $1.75. Value increases for celebrities. MIB. Courtesy Joanna Brunken.

Mutt from the *Noah's Ark* series, ca. 1970s: 3″/7.5 cm. long, grey wooly plush over a metal body, f.j., black and white googly eyes, black stitched nose, red felt tongue. The look of a mongrel dog has been cleverly captured in this small toy. Rare. Courtesy Dee Hockenberry.

Puppy from the *Noah's Ark* series: 2½″/6.4 cm. long; mohair over a metal body, f.j., black and white googly eyes; stitched nose/mouth; seldom seen member of the Ark. Among these many animals made (ca. 1970), the more common are: Elephant, rabbit, cat, Scottie and dressed duck. They were all individually packaged in a colorful box. Courtesy Dee Hockenberry.

Schuco Bears: Left, Soccer Player, 3½″/9 cm., 1970s mohair over metal head, pipe cleaner body, metal eyes, floss nose; dressed in felt uniform and plastic Adidas soccer shoes. These bears were dressed to represent the 12 German soccer teams. This one is from Munich and sports the team colors, as well as an emblem on his jersey which reads, "F.C. Bayern Munchen E.V."; rare. Eight miniatures: 2½″/6.4 cm. and 3½″/9 cm.: 1970s mohair over metal body, f.j., metal eyes, floss nose; 2 with original ribbons. Far right: Somersaulting Bear, 5″/12 cm., mohair over metal body, jointed arms, pin-jointed legs, glass eyes, felt pads on front feet, floss nose, original ribbon. He performs acrobatic somersaults when wound with key inserted in hole under right arm. Though non-working, he remains rare and appealing, ca. 1960-1970. Courtesy Kirk Stines.

IX. Teddy Bear Related Items

Old print or postcard in original frame, titled "Delighted"; copyright 1907, Gutmann & Gutmann. These pictures by prominent artists provide valuable information with exact dating as well as form a pleasing display in the "Teddy Bear Room." There were a vast number of prints, ca. 1910, just as there are today for greeting cards, etc. Courtesy Wanda Loukides.

"Billie Possum" 10″/25 cm., dark grey mohair, straw stuffed, f.j., shoe button eyes; felt ears and long felt tail. There is no chance of mistaking this animal for anything but an opossum. Possible maker, Character Novelty Co. Billy Possum, as a soft toy (1909), was an off-shoot of the Teddy Bear. Likewise, the possum's roots stemmed from a political incident: The then President-elect, William Howard Taft, came to consider the possum his personal emblem. Billy did *not* capture the public's imagination and soon disappeared from the scene; rare today and avidly sought by serious collectors who tend to want what they can't have. Shown with political postcard, coat button and silver spoon. Courtesy Helen Sieverling.

Two Teddy Bears in Toyland has charming *photographs* depicting the adventures of two mohair bears with dolls and toys from that period. Published in 1907 by Dodd, Mead & Co., NY. Extremely rare early book. Courtesy Carolyn Dockray.

German cardboard doll, 8½″/22 cm., who loves her Teddy Bear, ca. 1920. Purchased on the bank of the Seine in Paris. Courtesy Nan C. Moorehead.

Raphael Tuck mechanical embossed cardboard toy 11½″/29 cm. Pulling the string brings two arms up, ca. 1900. "Our Friends the Bears". "We are the three Bears come to call, The Big, the Middling and the Small; You'll see that really we are four, But thought you would not mind one more." Raphael Tuck & Sons, Ltd. Courtesy Nan C. Moorehead.

Child's silverplate spoon and fork set in lithographed box with Roosevelt-type Bear. Hard to find in original box, ca. 1915. Courtesy Wanda Loukides.

Turn-of-the-century candy containers are now an extension of soft toy collecting: 8″/20 cm. high, 12″/30.5 cm. long; the hunting dog is beautifully modelled of papier mache with a stitched covering of painted felt; removable head. Courtesy Diane Hoffman.

A little girl's dream, ca. 1910: 10″/25 cm., lush gold mohair, jointed head, glass eyes, feet dangle, no arms, original silk bow; all making him special and he knows it. Conformation of the Teddy Bear head indicates one of the earliest muffs. Mint condition. Courtesy Carolyn Dockray.

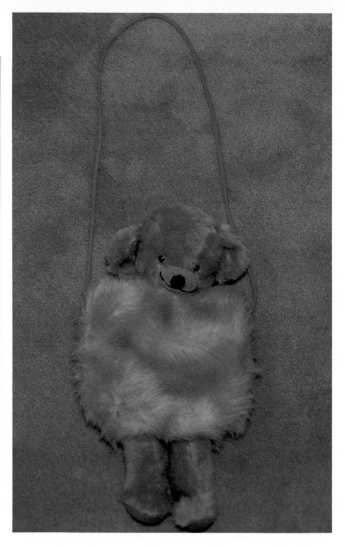

Cheeky muff, 13″/33 cm., gold deep pile mohair head and legs, cotton stuffed, orange/black glass eyes, black floss nose/mouth, orange velveteen snout, felt pads. Note *bells* in both ears; red rayon neck strap/also found on other Merrythought children's muffs, e.g. rabbits, lambs, etc. ca. 1960-1961. Courtesy Misty Tidwell.

Kitty cat rabbit fur muff: 7″/17.5 cm. high, 8″/20 cm. wide; white with black for ears and tail; straw stuffed disc jointed head, stitch jointed front legs; green glass eyes, black floss vertical nose; body is soft stuffed and lined with white rayon satin; early plastic carrying handle. From author's childhood, ca. 1930s.

"Ideal Baby Mine, U.S. Pat. Doll Muff No. 41179," 8½"/22 cm. x 12"/30.5 cm., thick white mohair, celluloid doll face with painted features, felt hands and feet; muff is padded with cotton. The Ideal Toy Corp. imported the head from Germany, ca. 1915. Mint. Courtesy Sammie Chambliss.

Royal Worcester bone china made in England: 6¾"/17 cm. high, "Wednesday's child knows little woe." Purchased a the factory in 1978; now discontinued. Courtesy Margot Mandel.

Pajama Bag Teddy: 14"/36 cm., sitting, gold mohair, straw stuffed head, kapok stuffed limbs jointed by wire armature; brown glass eyes; black floss nose/mouth, no claws; tan painted canvas pads; zippered back with pink satin lining. Tag sewn on right leg, "Farnell Alpha, Hygenic Soft Toy, Made in England." Note the sweet English face, ca. 1950. Courtesy Dee Hockenberry.

Large paper dolls, ca. 1916: Full color lithograph with Teddy 7″/17.5 cm.; named "Dottie Mae's Paper Fun" because they were the childhood toys of Dottie Mae born in 1907. Courtesy Virginia Joy.

Older Teddy Bear related items are becoming scarce. Bear Brand Hosiery box: 10″/25 cm. x 6¼″/16 cm.; stamped on bottom, "Aug. 18, 1921." The jig-saw puzzle has always been one of the most popular "quiet" games for children. Puzzle: 9½″/24 cm. x 7½″/19 cm., paper-covered masonite; made in U.S.A. by Whitman Publishing Co., ca. 1912. (Author).

Roosevelt Bear metal bank, 6″/15 cm., coin slot in back of head. Tape Measure Bear, 2½″/6.4 cm., reddish brown plush over a hard form, glass eyes, blue ribbon; pull tail to use tape measure; paper label on bottom, "Made in Japan"; ca. 1920. Bottom, Teddy Bear clothes buttons, ¾″/2 cm., brass, ca. 1915. Courtesy Wanda Loukides.

Teddy Bears and Valentines seem to go together; both date from 1930-1940. Collectors with limited funds find satisfaction in searching for this worthwhile ephemera that can still be found. Teddy: 20″/51 cm.; gold mohair; f.j.; glass eyes; black floss nose/mouth on nicely projected snout; felt pads; squeaker. Courtesy Marlene Wendt.

Jessie Wilcox Smith, "Goldilocks"; 9"/23 cm. x 12"/30.5 cm. (page size, 12"/30.5 cm. x 15"/38 cm.); not a photographic reproduction but an *actual page* from her book, enhances value. Courtesy Brenda Hoyle.

Hamm's Beer, Madison Avenue's "best" bear face; popular advertising bear accessories give spark to a collection: Large is plastic sign: medium bear is bottle with removable head; small is glass salt shaker, ca. 1950s. Courtesy Roberta Viscusi.

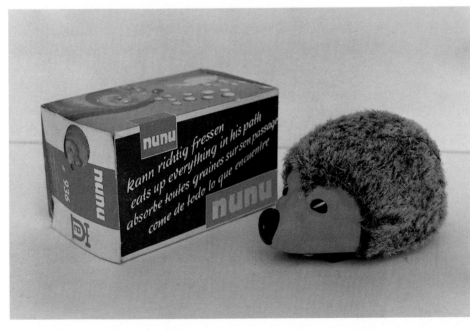

Friction toy, 6"/15 cm., painted metal face (eats everything in its path); synthetic hair covering of a hedgehog, an old world mammal having both hair and spines similar to the American porcupine. Made by the prestigious Lehman Co., marked "NUNU, 936, International Patents Pend., Made in Western Germany"; applicable to the "Mecki Family" mystique. Courtesy Diane Hoffman.

Steiff stuffed animals courtesy of F.A.O. Schwarz as seen in *Coats & Clarks Book No. 167*, knit and crochet patterns for children 1966. This ephemra is fun to look for and far cheaper than the animals. (Author).

Left, an artist's Golliwog, 15″/38 cm. If you can't go to England, make your own Golliwog. This Golliwog was made from a commercial pattern. The body is made of Zeus, a rayon satin-finished coat lining that is stable; polyfill stuffed; unjointed although arms and legs are attached pieces and Golliwog is capable of sitting. Unique features are his long nose, which most Golliwogs (except the 1913, Steiff) don't have and his feather boa hair. Dressed in the traditional colors of a British National, the clothes are all removable. Middle: New Kathe Kruse unjointed bear. 8″/20 cm. He keeps the Golliwogs occupied or is it the other way around. Right: 18½″/47 cm. made by Merrythought Ltd. Golliwog's long wild hair gives him a creative look. Note typical Merrythought construction of hands and feet. Clothes cannot be removed. In 1949 Merrythought advertised their traditional Golliwog as "Jolliwog." All courtesy Mary Alice Carey.

Left, Golliwog, 18½″/47 cm. made by Merrythought Ltd. of England. Face and hands are synthetic short pile fabric, similar to velveteen. Mitten-like hands have stitched fingers. Orange velvet top and aqua plain weave cotton pants make the body. Feet are yellow broadcloth and brown velveteen. Chest has noisemaker inside. Golliwog designs from the major companies change periodically; the discontinued increase in value. Middle, 11″/28 cm. Another Merrythought Golliwog with formal "tails" and wonderful long, carefree hair. Note similar design features in the hands and feet of the two Merrythought Golliwogs, ca. 1978. Right, 16″/41 cm., made by Gabrielle Designs Ltd., Doncaster, England; tagged in right leg seam covered by black and white cotton pants. Coat is red felt with "tails." He sports a white lace dickey; black and white polka dot bowtie. All clothing can be removed. Body is a cotton twill; hair is a thick soft synthetic fur. "Quality" best describes every detail, ca. 1980. All courtesy Mary Alice Carey.

The Golliwog, the Teddy Bear's best friend, was created by illustrator, Florence Kate Upton in 1895. Bertha Upton, Florence's mother, wrote the verse for the dozen or so children's books that they published in England around the turn of the century. In general, the Golliwog is formally dressed in "tails." He is to represent a British National and traditionally—but not always—his attire is red, white and blue. You will see other colors used such as orange, aqua and yellow. They are difficult to find in the United States. Golliwog, 12½"/32 cm., I.D. cloth tag sewn into center back seam, "Dean's Childplay Toys Ltd., Rye, Sussex, England." The clothes and face with unusual expressive eyes are printed on the fabric. Child's breakfast dishes: Plate and bowl, 6½"/16 cm. diameter; marked "Royal Swan, Made in England." The lucky owner of these dishes enjoyed the company of Golliwogs at every breakfast (late 1940s, early 1950s). Egg cup and saucer are missing. All courtesy Karen Watson.

Valentine, printed in Germany: The loveboat has a Teddy Bear in the bow and a Golliwog in the stern. Passenger sends greetings of love to a friend. Golliwog ephemera is hard to find and very collectible. Golliwog, 12½"/32 cm., no I.D.: Synthetic plush hair and printed facial features; foam rubber stuffed; nylon coat/"tails" and striped pants; black nylon knit shoes; clothes cannot be removed, ca. 1970s. Unusual and older Golliwogs are in great demand. All these Golliwogs keep the chocolate brown, long mohair Teddy Bear company until play time. Bear, 15"/38 cm., was purchased in 1945 by owner's mother. Cloth tag in center seam, "Knickerbocker Toy Co., Inc. New York." Right, small play mugs, 3"/7 cm.: These mugs served as great advertisements and promotional medium for the James Robertson Company, maker of "Golden Shred - the world's best orange jelly marmalade." The paper coupons seen in front of the mugs were redeemed for Golliwog items such as these mugs. All courtesy Mary Alice Carey.

Dolls With Teddy Bears

Jenny Lind singing to her Schuco cat from the *Noah's Ark* series: 2½"/6.4 cm. long; mohair/tabby stripes, black mohair ears and tail; f.j.; green eyes; floss nose/mouth; nylon whiskers; original blue neck ribbon. Doll: 14"/36 cm., made by Madame Alexander (1969-1970). Piano decoration is an older jointed wooden bear. Courtesy Chris McWilliams.

Peter Bull, Father of the Teddy Bear Movement and a celebrity in his own right: beloved friend to many and an inspiration to all: Portrait doll (in memoriam), 8"/20 cm., styrene composition, wearing his famed pull-over; made in 1986 by the House of Nisbet in a Limited Edition of 5,000 worldwide. Issue price, $75.00; appears to be a good candidate for appreciation. Courtesy Rosemary Moran.

Display loosely titled, "Peaceable Kindom," after the American master folk artist Edward Hicks' 1850s paintings to illustrate sermons and Bible stories. King "Leo," 20"/50 cm. long, No. 2350, orange glass lion's eyes set in the beautifully marked mohair head; straw and kapok stuffed; rose twisted floss nose, black floss mouth and claws; heavy nylon filament whiskers. Mint/C.T. and Steiff button. "Lamby," 8½"/20 cm. high, white wool plush, straw stuffed, green glass eyes, red floss nose/mouth; felt lined ears, ca. 1950. Doll, 28"/71 cm., closed mouth Kestner, No. 698/12. (Author).

The mark of German quality: 24″/61 cm., lying Boxer and Spaniel made by FECO, ca. late 1970s; short pile synthetic plush, molded hard plastic noses; brown plastic eyes/white heavy felt backing (iris-shape), painted above, rimmed below with leatherette giving depth. Beautifully decorated in a life-like style, it is reported that the art director of FECO is a former Steiff employee. Marked "FECO, Made in Germany." Lenci doll, 20″/51 cm., painted flirting eyes, tagged taffeta long dress. (Author).

Collecting Eloise Wilkin could be an all consuming hobby in itself. Her illustrated books are greatly admired and many have been reissued. *My Teddy Bear*, copyright 1953 by Golden Press, Inc. together with the Vogue Doll Co. "Too Dear," a cherubic, pudgy, 2 year old toddler (1963). Her Teddy (not original to doll) is 7½″/19 cm., brown cotton plush, soft stuffed, unjointed; plastic disc eyes, *red felt tongue* (typifies Gund), ca. 1950. (Author).

Mattel's Dreamtime Barbie with her cuddly bear, "B.B.": 11½″/29 cm., super star face; made in Taiwan (1984). The Teddy Bear craze prompted Mattel to produce Barbie (always in step with the times) with the pink bear she loves to hug; a popular seller. Courtesy Kim Rehor.

"Lori 'N Rori" from Mattel's 1969-1970 "Pretty Pairs." Lori is Tutti size, 6¼"/16 cm.; Rori is 2½"/6.4 cm., brown synthetic plush; brown painted fur and blue eyes on the jointed head; yellow felt tie, yellow felt ear linings on the removable plush Teddy Bear cap; original pink ribbon bow. A tiny treasure easily lost; doll/bear is extremely scarce, mint. (Author).

Jan Hagara's "Cristina," 15"/38 cm., made by Effanbee from the print of the same name. Her bear, "Edward Theodore," was designed by Linda Spiegel of Bearly There Co., a Limited Edition in the amount ordered during a 2 year period. The first 1,000 tags have the doll's name mispelled, "Christina." Bear: 6"/15 cm., gold upholstery velvet; f.j.; 5 mm. black wooden bead eyes; black floss horizontal nose/mouth, 3 claws; narrow burgundy grosgrain neck ribbon; tagged and numbered; 1983. (Author).

"Michael" with Schuco miniature Teddy Bear (seen elsewhere). In 1969 Madame Alexander made the Walt Disney Peter Pan Set of 4 dolls: "Peter Pan," "Wendy," "Tinker Bell" and "Michael," Of these, "Michael" is the most popular because of his Teddy Bear and the favored Janie face mold, 11"/28 cm., in shocking pink jersey jump suit. (Author).

Goldilocks (Madame Alexander 1978) and three Gebr. Hermann KG bears of that year. Papa, 15″/38 cm., gold mohair, straw and cotton stuffed, f.j., plastic eyes, black floss nose/mouth; peach *jersey* pads; growler. Mama, 12″/30.5 cm., same as above; no voice box; discontinued light blonde color mohair. Baby, 8″/20 cm., gold mohair. All are sweet bears as Hermanns tend to be. Dressed by owner. (Author).

Courtesy Gebrueder Hermann KG, Catalog, ca. 1970s. Note how recently Gebr. Hermann made Teddy Bears with an inset long snout of sheared mohair. This feature is found on their earlier models as well.

Animals From Fiction

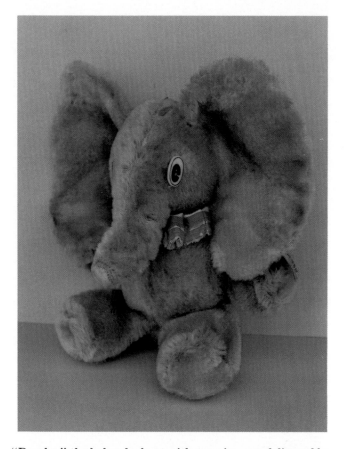

"Dumbo," the baby elephant with oversize ears delivered by the stork to a circus performer. He is the butt of jokes until he learns how to fly: 12″/30.5 cm., thick grey mohair, unjointed, celluloid pie-shaped (cartoon) eyes, felt nose; tied on neck ruff (missing blue felt hat with a white pom-pom). Rayon tag on left ear, "Dumbo, the Flying Elephant, copyright Walt Disney Productions; Character Novelty Co. Licensee, South Norwalk, Conn." ca. 1940. (Author).

"Krazy Kat": 19″/48 cm., kelly green felt, unjointed, machine appliqued white felt face with cut-out eyes and mouth, red felt foot pads and bowtie; extra long straw stuffed tail. Cotton tag sewn into back seam below neck, "KRAZY KAT", manufactured under special arrangement with Geo. Herriman, patent applied for, Averill Mfg. Co., 37 Union Sq., W.N.Y."; drawing of comic character on reverse side. Extremely rare and in mint condition, 1916. "Ignatz", 5½″/14 cm., segmented wood, white pipe cleaner stem tail. Stamped on foot, "Made in U.S.A." Courtesy Margot Mandel.

"Ferdinand": 12″/30.5 cm. high, 14″/36 cm. long, black cotton plush body, yellow mohair belly, white mohair topknot, straw stuffed head and legs, cotton stuffed body, unjointed; celluloid disc eyes, velveteen nose with stitch to hold (missing) flower; pink velveteen-lined ears; white velveteen horns and forehead; beige cotton twill feet; mohair bee is sewn at tail. Rare, ca. 1930s. *The Story of Ferdinand* by Munro Leaf illustrated by Robert Lawson, September 1936. (Author).

Chloe Preston's famous creation "Dinkie" made by Merrythought (1936-1959): 3½″/9 cm. high, jointed head only, rust color velveteen with inset gold markings, unusual glass eyes (shank type), finely embroidered nose, white felt tongue; came in other beautiful art shades of velvet. A similar pin cushion dog is seen in Steiff's 1927 catalog. To further tangle the identification, this example appears identical to the Bonzo dog in the 1927 Gebr. Hermann catalog. (Author).

Bugs Bunny, part of Americana: 16″/40.5 cm., all felt, hard stuffed cotton, jointed by wire armature, painted mask face, original pink felt collar, silk ribbon tie; tagged "Bugs Bunny, Warner Bros. Cartoons, Inc." One of the many examples of this successful animated character, ca. 1940-1950. Courtesy Colleen Ripley.

Maker unknown: 15″/38 cm., cotton/mohair plush, kapok stuffed, unjointed, early vinyl face with painted features. Goes well with *The Road to Oz* by L. Frank Baum (1937). Courtesy Kay Bransky.

121

Winnie-the-Pooh, central character in the set made and distributed by Agnes Brush, Whitestone, L.I., with permission of Stephen Slesinger, Inc.: 13″/33 cm., tan flannel, kapok stuffed, black felt nose, black bead eyes, original red wool jersey knit sweater. One cannot deny the pleasing simplicity of this Pooh ca. early 1960s. Courtesy Kelly Tidwell.

Chad Valley dog "Bonzo"; 13″/33 cm., 1930s velvet (velveteen), soft stuffed, f.j., airbrushed eyes, velvet nose, felt pacifier in mouth (usually lost), embroidered claws; feet have cardboard innersoles; label on left foot, "Hygienic Toys, Made in England by Chad Valley Co. Ltd."; note the airbrushed markings remain clear and distinct. Extremely rare. Posed with reproduction of Bonzo postcard by original designer, G.E. Studdy. Bonzo was a popular cartoon character that originated in the 1920s. Steiff made a printed velvet Bonzo (ca. 1930s) in 2 models: Standing with swivel head and a fully jointed version in 8″/20 cm. and 13½″/34 cm. sizes. From 1952-1954 Merrythought also produced Bonzo, 9″/23 cm., in velvet with painted features. That dog had a black velvet nose and no pacifier. Courtesy Kirk Stines.

"Daisy" from the comic strip *Blondie* created by Chic Young: 9″/23 cm. high, 8″/20 cm. long, thick gold mohair, straw stuffed, jointed head, glass eyes/black felt backing; velvet stuffed nose; long feet and distinctive ears and tail. Since comic strip art and jazz music are the only purely American contributions to art, these early examples of comic characters must be treasured, ca. 1950. Courtesy Rosemary Moran.

The First "Snoopy": 8″/20 cm., high (made in 3 sizes), early vinyl, black painted features with pie-shaped eyes; squeaker; marked on bottom; "United Feature Syndicate, 1958." Note how time has changed the configuration of the Beagle. This 1958 Snoopy is not self-recognizable and could be overlooked. Courtesy Margot Mandel.

Pooh and Eeyore from patterns: one of many issued over the years. Some were unauthorized and withdrawn from the market; 10″/25 cm. crochet with felt features; 14″/36 cm. synthetic plush Pooh, sewn-on felt features, red corduroy sweater; Eeyore, 15″/38 cm., grey knit jersey, cream knit jersey underside; once had a button-on tail. Various books of the A.A. Milne classic are the foundation for this favorite collection, ca. 1970. Courtesy Bill Gardner. In time the homemade examples will be valuable.

Paddington and Aunt Lucy, 18″/46 cm., show the universal appeal and staying power of Teddy Bears. This pair is not for export to U.S.; Paddington was made in England (1972) by Gabrielle Designs for distribution only in England, Australia, New Zealand, Malaysia and The Netherlands. The white synthetic plush has a cashmere-feel and is hard stuffed with cotton making a substantial bear; unjointed, yellow plastic eyes, blue felt coat, red hat/safety pin, heavy vinyl Wellington boots. Aunt Lucy came into being in 1978; long pile synthetic plush, brown plastic eyes rimmed with vinyl. Note: the right leg of her pantaloons has a pocket in which there are 2 coins stamped, "Home for Retired Bears, Lima, Darkest Peru"; safety pin closure on shawl. Aunt Lucy is hard to find even in the slightly altered U.S. version currently made by *Eden*. Choice early examples of a remarkable pair. Courtesy Pam Johnson.

Jungle Book, Walt Disney's 1967 motion picture inspired by Rudyard Kipling's *All the Mowgli Stories* (1894), presented the world with a cast of loveable creatures that Steiff converted from screen images to delightful play companions. The story is that of Mowgli, the "man-cub," who was orphaned and raised by wolves in the jungle of India. The boy is guided by Bagheera, the panther; entertained by Baloo, the bear; plays with a little elephant, Baby Hathi; acquaints himself with King Louie, monarch of the apes and is stalked by the sly and treacherous Shere Khan, the tiger. "Baloo," 16"/40 cm., No. 0360/40, beige Dralon, jointed head and arms; made from 1968-1974 and 1979-1982. Higher value can be attached to him because a *bear*. "King Louie," 10"/25 cm., No. 0050/25, shades of brown Crylor, jointed head, dangling arms. (1968-1974 and 1979-1982). He and Baby Hathi are the most common of the set. "Baby Hathi," 8"/20 cm., No. 0530/20, grey Dralon, unjointed, standing. He has the longest production life (1968-1975 with a dark grey plush turning to a lighter grey 1979-1982). Courtesy David McWilliams.

"Bagheera," 10"/25 cm., No. 0381/25, glistening black plush (60% acrylic, 40% cotton), white inset snout, pink jersey nose outlined in floss, painted mouth, yellow plastic eyes, *black* nylon wiskers. Outstanding contouring. A substitute for "Shere Khan" in the 1979-1982 set. Among the many avid collectors of *Jungle Book*, "Bagheera" is usually the last to be found. An example of: most recent can also be most rare. (Author).

"Shere Khan," 13½"/35 cm., No. 0920/35, orange/white tiger striped Dralon, jointed head. Originally catalogued as a "Novelty"; now a great treasure because he was loved to death by children. Note the smirk on the superb face; an excellent example of Steiff sculpturing in a soft toy (1968-1974). Courtesy Carolyn Altfather.

Hedgehog-type figures: all 3⅜″/9 cm. tall, mohair wig, vinyl head with painted features, jointed by bendable wire in vinyl body; hard plastic shoes marked, "Made in Korea." The fragile wire construction is easily broken by a child as well as being dangerous. Sixteen examples called "Collectible, irrespressible Mackys: Wacky Mackys" appear in Steiff's 1978 catalogue. However, Steiff denies association with them. They are also seen in a color catalogue from Austria where they are called, "Original Peter; *Handarbeit*," and shown in 50 different trade and sport costumes. Each of the miniatures show amazing detail and have an average of 3 accessories each; for example the Backpacker carries a pack, flowers and an ice axe. The sets are all touched with humor and boxed as "Original Peter, Made in Republic of Korea." Some boxes are stamped inside, "July 4, 1976." Currently they are flooding the market. (Author).

German language child's story book: *Mein groBes Igel-Buch* by Helene Weilen published 1961 in Munich. Anny Hoffman's many fine color illustrations depict the Mecki Family (described in Vol. I) in day to day activities. (Author).

Capt'n Joshua of the USS Happiness crew: 12″/30.5 cm., honey-beige plush, unjointed, gold velvet pads; note the all-embroidered features including beautifully done *eyes*. Tagged "USS Happiness Crew tm. 1979 Determined Products, Inc., San Francisco CA"; came in three sizes, 19″/48 cm., 12″/30.5 cm. and 7½″/19 cm. Taken from June Dutton's book *Capt'n Joshua's Dangerous Dilemma* published by Determined Production. Other characters in the stories were Tasha (elephant), Jack (rabbit), Dr. Phineas (frog), Allie (cat) and Wrecker (racoon). All in a limited production, one year only. Retail of 12″/30.5 cm. was $9.95 in 1979. Norah Welling's sailor, 7½″/19 cm., papier mache head, all cloth body with celluloid shoes. Courtesy Virginia Joy.

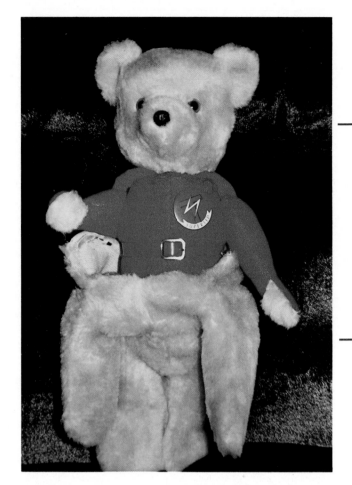

Original Super Ted from England (1982): 16″/41 cm., zip-off synthetic fur covering reveals a fully jointed Teddy Bear in his Superman-like suit. An example of another important character bear from across the sea. In 1985 *R. Dakin & Co.* produced this familiar TV cartoon personality in 10¼″/26 cm. and 15″/38 cm. sizes; f.j., the plush bear suit zips off to a red caped outfit enabling him to fly about the world solving crimes. Courtesy Roberta Viscusi.

Popular German TV character: Little Green Man *(Grunes Mannchen)*; 13½″/35 cm., No. 7885/35, green (100% polyester) knit body similar to "Cappy" dangling frog, hard stuffed, painted pink jersey open mouth, 2 white felt teeth, black elastic antennae; large black/white hard plastic eyes; leatherette freestanding eyebrows; incised brass button (5⁄16″). He was for the German market only 1982-1984; a purely decorative manniken created by the Belgian artist Mallet; a mascot to bring smiles. Rare. (Author).

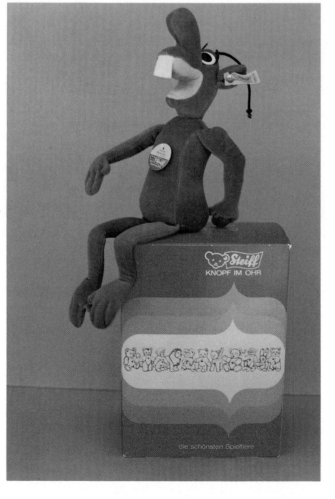

Advertising Bears & Puppets

Kellogs Co., Battle Creek, Michigan,; "Daddy Bear," 13"/33 cm., "Mama Bear," 12"/30.5 cm., "Johnny Bear," 10"/25 cm., "Goldilocks," 12"/30.5 cm.; printed cotton stuffed with cotton batting; given as a company premium for advertising, ca. 1925. This is the first issue where the "Daddy Bear" has green trousers with navy stripes; in 1926 they were changed to red and yellow striped. Rare to have the first issue with *four* mint figures. Value must be increased for complete sets. Today's advertising bears may appreciate a thousand times in 50 years as these have. Courtesy Sammie Chambliss.

Teddy Baby hand puppet: 10"/25 cm., brown mohair, tan mohair snout, brown glass eyes, black twisted floss nose/mouth, beige floss claws, open mouth; original red ribbon, ca. 1950-1970s. Center: 8½"/22 cm., older Steiff; light brown mohair, straw stuffed head, brown glass eyes, black twisted floss nose/mouth and claws, no pads; note the pointed snout. Right: 9"/23 cm., made by Felpa (Swiss); tan mohair, hard stuffed head, brown glass eyes, black floss nose/mouth and claws; peach felt pads. Courtesy Wanda Loukides.

Hand puppets, all 6½"/17 cm.: "Lora" Parrot, No. 6685/17, exotic coloring of the mohair, straw stuffed head, plastic "glow-in-the-dark" *rimmed* eyes; incised button; made 1968-1977. Boy "Hansel", No. 7071/17, vinyl head, mohair hair; felt and flannel clothes (missing green cap and red scarf); felt hands; made early 1970s-1978. Alligator "Gaty", No. 6970/17, mohair, straw stuffed head, plastic "glow-in-the-dark" rimmed eyes, open felt mouth and teeth. Note a newer chest tag would be fastened with nylon filament instead of thread. Made from mid-1950s to 1978. The useful Steiff display stands are provided at the discretion of the dealer. Courtesy Kirk Stines.

Complete sets of Steiff Hide-a-Gift animals: 6"/15 cm.; head and arms are mohair, except the fox and bear which are Dralon ("Bayer" brand synthetic fiber that is wear resistant). Hollow felt skirts to hide small gifts; jointed head only. The rabbits (came in four different outfits) are more common; the other individual animals are harder to find and came only in color as shown. Some have raised script, prong-attached buttons; others have incised rivet-attached buttons; showing once again that all identification standards were not changed the same year, ca. early 1970s. Courtesy Jane L. Viprino.

"Musicians of Bremen," finger play puppets: 2½"/06 cm., No. 7080/06, felt and wool. The complete set of four includes: Donkey, dog, cat and rooster. Hard to find in original plastic box with Steiff buttons, ca. 1968. Courtesy Jane L. Viprino.

Hershey Teddy Bear "Kisses"; 5"/12.5 cm., retains the original chocolate smell; chocolate brown synthetic plush, soft stuffed, unjointed; brown plastic eyes, yarn nose/mouth, removable sweater; tagged "Ideal Toy Co.", ca. 1982, cost $3.50. "Tuffy" tagged right foot, "Master Industries, St. Paul, Minn., A Master Product." Length, 14"/36 cm., grey/white short pile synthetic plush, well decorated and contoured, soft stuffed (legs have wire armature); unjointed, brown glass eyes/dark brown felt backing and eyebrows, black pom-pom nose, red felt tongue; removable purple knit sweater, ca. 1960. (Author).

Jolly Fox: 19½"/50 cm., No. 3482/50, luxurious Dralon, soft stuffed arm puppet; yellow plastic eyes, leatherette nose; painted mouth; whiskers; black Trevira velvet pads; wonderful face. Jolly animals serve as both arm puppets and bedtime animals, ca. 1975-1978 (short production but little demand). Cost $52.00 in 1975. Steiff hopping rabbit: 4½"/11.5 cm. high, brown/white mohair, raised script button, *cloth* I.D. tag, ca. 1950-1960. (Author).

Pillsbury Co. "Cupcake": 14"/36 cm., white plush, soft stuffed, unjointed; unusual bright blue flat plastic eyes, blue pompom nose and blue stitched mouth. The original bib is usually missing, ca. 1974. Advertising bears are a good specualtion and fun to acquire. Courtesy Roberta Viscusi.

Premium Teddy Bear given out by Crocker National Bank (California) for opening a savings account of $500.00 or more. Excellent design by Animal Fair, Inc.: 16"/41 cm., thick rust color plush, unjointed, soft stuffed, black plush nose, red felt mouth; came in blue/white striped tee shirt but lends itself well to any outfit. Hard to find outside of California, ca. 1975. Courtesy Roberta Viscusi.

Advertising bears are bought by serious collectors. As they become scarce, their prices will be based on speculation: 16"/40.5 cm., "Big Pink" lettered "Owens-Corning Fiberglass" on sewn-to-body blue overalls. Pink synthetic fur; wonderful expression on the long snout. Made in 1979 by Animal Fair who is noted for outstanding design. Some soil and matting. Hard to find. (Author).

Made by Steiff exclusively for advertising the Commerzbank, Germany: 13½"/34 cm., gold Dralon; fluff surrounding snout, red Trevira velvet open mouth; two felt teeth; pink plastic nose and bulging black hard plastic eyes; 12 black whiskers; black Trevira velvet lined ears. Dressed in removable yellow cotton pants and shirt printed with the bank's logo and "Goldi" hamster. Large brass button with yellow *paper* (not cloth) I.D. tag No. 7955/32; reverse side is "Commerzbank" and their logo. This cheerful hamster caused traffic problems at the bank in 1985. Courtesy Beth Savino, Hobby Center Toys.

X. Steiff Dolls

Rolly Polly clown: 10″/25 cm., printed Steiff button "ff" underscored, center seam on felt face, bright blue tiny glass eyes; hair is inset blonde curly mohair, wonderful felt hands with separate fingers; complete silk velvet clown outfit (often the hat or ruff is missing); normal wear to the delicate velvet. Note the "sweet little boy look" found on other character dolls from 1913. That year Steiff made the same style Rolly Pollys depicting comic men, cats, rabbits and bears. Without a doubt, the simplest toys are best for children. By the second half of the 19th century, a Rolly Polly doll had been made on an industrial scale. In 1908 A. Schoenhut & Co. (an American firm established in 1872) patented the "Rolly Dolly." These were made of wood in different designs and sizes. Steiff adapted the concept to their own construction methods. Rare and desirable example of a Steiff doll. Courtesy Beth Savino, Hobby Center Toys.

"Humpty Dumpty," 10″/25 cm. tall, head circumference 20″/51 cm., all felt with painted features, straw filled, jointed limbs, oversize shoe button eyes; no Steiff button but *stamped* with Steiff's registered trademark, "Knopf im Ohr" on the bottom of left foot. The Steiff enthusiast would be lucky to find this favorite nursery rhyme character today. Mint, ca. 1913. Rare. Courtesy Robin Lowe.

Witch in caricature: 17″/43 cm., straw stuffed, f.j., seam down center face, black shoe button eyes; hair is inset mohair, separate fingers curl around the original cane. Designed in 1912 by A. Schlopsnies for the Steiff firm, she is a masterpiece in understatement; note the prominent witch-like chin and nose. The exaggerated cheek bones retain the original blushing. All original clothing includes the black brimmed witch's hat with a dark blue peak. Printed Steiff button "ff" underscored. Mint. Considered by many to be the most collectible Steiff toys: (1) Early dolls with felt face and center seam; (2) Early Original Teddies; (3) Early wheeled animals. Courtesy Beth Savino, Hobby Center Toys.

"Gendarme": 11½″/29 cm., printed Steiff button "ff" underscored, straw stuffed, f.j., felt face/center seam, shoe button eyes, painted moustache, stitched fingers; red stripes on sides of black trousers. Correct in every detail, the outfit portrays one of the many individual policemen of the time; missing one epaulet and brass buttons from jacket. This durable doll was designed to give a child the possibility of fantasizing himself as a policeman. They were thought to be suitable for boys, ca. 1913. Now a rare display piece. Excellent condition. Courtesy Robin Lowe.

Morphology of a Steiff character child, ca. 1913: 14″/35.5 cm., seam down center of face and from eye to sewn-on ear (to facilitate modelling); tiny periwinkle blue glass eyes, blonde mohair fastened onto a backing and set into head; painted mouth that is lightly stitched for form, nose is also shaped by small stitches. There are center seams, front and back, of both legs and arms as well as torso. Pink threads define fingers on the somewhat clumsy mitten hands; firmly stuffed with straw; swivel head, disc jointed arms and legs. See her dressed as the Tyrolean "Lizzie."

Tyrolean "Lizzie," 14″/35.5 cm.; also made in a 11″/28 cm. size. There is more demand for the larger size. Dressed in green felt skirt/black braid trim, wide black felt waistband draped with crystal beads, white cotton apron, blouse, undies and slip; all are handstitched; tweed knit half-socks; sturdy black felt shoes. Missing are hat, waistcoat and one shoe. Steiff button "ff" underscored. These dolls were manufactured in large numbers, but with the ravages of time, insects and war, they are difficult to find in good condition. Mohair baby boar: 4″/10 cm., No. 2670/10, ca. 1970. Note the blue (plastic) eyes to match the doll's. Courtesy Carl R. McQueary.

"Struwelpeter" catalogued as "Mop-head" in 1913, the hey-day of Steiff dolls. "Strewelpeter" is derived from the legend of a straggly headed, unkempt little boy with long unclean fingernails. In Germany this name came to be the term for any naughty little boy. Note, he has a child's face and a comic's body: 12″/30.5 cm., a seam down the middle of the felt face and laterally from the eye to the ear; black button eyes; extra long hair is inset mohair; wonderful construction detail of the important large hands with long inset orange fingernails (only one remains, otherwise doll is mint and all original); printed button "ff" underscored. Rare. Courtesy Beth Savino, Hobby Center Toys.

Dutchman "Olaf," 14″/36 cm. (one size only). See "Lizzie" for description. Ethnic costume: Hunter green pouf-type felt pants with white pearl button trim on front waistband. This waistband snaps to the felt jacket; note the top stitched lapels. The cotton shirt is white/red stripe pattern (hook and eye closure), red collar studded with 2 brass buttons; a brass button trims lapel; crocheted dark brown cotton socks; beige felt Dutch shoe/upturned toe. Missing hat. The photograph of the Kaiser has always been with him. Courtesy Carl R. McQueary.

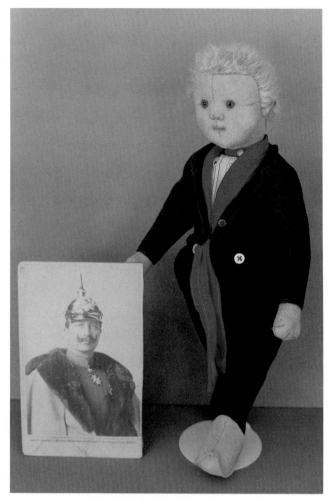

The allure of the Steiff doll: Moor, 22″/56 cm.; printed button with *yellow* paper I.D. tag on wrist band indicates that he is from late 1930s. It is unusual to find anything but character children from this period. The large size is extraordinary for Steiff; the play doll averaged 13″/33 cm. The hard composition-type head with mohair beard is also unexpected. The Moor is a well balanced design that is beautifully decorated; note the unusual scabbard and flowing lines to the robes. The *large* flat feet enable the doll to stand; the body construction is similar to other nationals (also large), ca. 1913; for example, Chinaman, Mexican etc. A rare treasure to spark the imagination of the child and collector alike. Add value because black dolls are avidly sought. It is thought that there was a large camel available as a companion piece. Mint. Courtesy Beth Savino, Hobby Center Toys.

1930s period: 16″/40.5 cm., straw stuffed, f.j., pressed felt face molded over a form, painted red lips and blue eyes with highlights, inset mohair wig, stitched fingers with separate thumb. Printed tiny button "ff" underscored. Dolls of this era were meant to awaken in the child a feeling for German womanhood and love of family. The value is decreased for replaced clothes. Courtesy Diane Hoffman.

Fireman doll made as a promotion piece for a German fire company, ca. 1980s: 15″/38 cm., incised brass button/paper I.D. tag,; a caricature in vinyl (note the bulbous nose); made with the same attention to detail as the early models (note the oversize feet, the Steiff buttons decorating the hatchet and double belt which is the trademark of the German fire brigade, the rope hanging at back of belt). It would be a challenge to build a collection around *all* of the Steiff advertising/promotional pieces. Hard to find in U.S.A. Courtesy Beth Savino, Hobby Center Toys.

Santa Claus: Large, 12½″/32 cm., straw stuffed, f.j.; felt with polyvinyl chloride (PVC) head which can deteriorate; mohair beard on the jovial face; dressed in the traditional red suit with white trimmings (90% wool, 10% rayon). Raised script button and old C.T., ca. early 1950s to early 1960s. Small, 7″/18 cm., same as above and also rare. Hand puppet, 12″/30.5 cm., dates from the same era and is hard to find. Steiff produced a small number of an *unjointed* Santa Claus, ca. late 1970s. His belt was riveted with Steiff buttons. In 1984-1985 Santa was reissued with a yellow *cloth* I.D. tag. The Christmas theme is popular with collectors. Courtesy Beth Savino, Hobby Center Toys.

"Max and Moritz," German comic characters from the cartoon books of Wilhelm Busch (1832-1908). Polyvinyl chloride (PVC), 3½"/9 cm.; jointed by bendable wire armature; painted features with side-glancing (googly) eyes, ca. 1960. Steiff first offered these favorite comics in an all-felt doll, ca. 1913. They have been made by Kammer & Reinhardt as bisque-headed googly dolls (also exceedingly rare) as well as by the American Schoenhut Co. All-bisque nodders can be found. Courtesy Robin Lowe.

"Clownie," 7½"/19 cm., No. 719, molded head is polyvinyl chloride (the original unstable formula has been perfected), painted clown features, straw stuffed felt body/limbs, f.j., cotton clothes; felt hat, shoes and gloves. A more recent doll inspired by the circus theme recurrent in Steiff's history; ca. 1950s on. Mint. Courtesy Dee Hockenberry.

"Cappy," 11"/28 cm., No. 7760/28, soft body for cuddling, vinyl head with painted features and inset plastic eyes, plush wig, blue and red silky suit with bells; felt hat, gloves and shoes. One size only. The sandman, "Sandy," used the same head mold, ca. 1970. Courtesy Dee Hockenberry.

XI. The German Village

"The Mill," part of the German Village assembled over a span of time by the Margarete Steiff Co. for display at the Century of Progress Exposition, Chicago (1933). The various exhibits of this World's Fair were regarded as the best ever asembled in the United States up to that time. Afterwards, the village went on tour of the U.S. ending up in a St. Paul, Minnesota, department store window for Christmas and subsequently was "lost" in storage. The amazing complex was purchased ca. 1935-1937 by the far-sighted father of the present owner, John R. Fazendin. The scenic photographs were made in 1956, the last time he set up the mechanical village. Since there was no "floor plan", John Fazendin had to deduce the general positioning and occupations of the figures. He painted the Tyrolean backdrop for this remarkable and unique treasure. There are two villages with a total of eighty figures. The "Animal Village" has nineteen mechanical animals; eighteen non-mechanical animals; seventeen of the total animal population are dressed as humans. The "German Village" houses ten mechanical dolls and thirty-three non-mechanical dolls. The mill structure (6 ft.) is in itself extraordinary. The paintwork and furnishings are original and beautifully made to an almost faultless scale. Every section is arranged as a fascinating scene.

The men of the German Village range in height from 15″/38 cm. to 17″/43 cm. All are self-standing on their elongated feet with leather shoes; all have a seam down the center face enabling the formation of the exaggerated profiles for which Steiff is so well known. Note the various distinctive chins, noses and foreheads-as well as the defined hands with stitched fingers and separate thumbs. They retain their original cheek blushing and lip color and have never been played with. Originating from the masterful hand of the artist, Albert Schlopsnies, each villager expresses a naive humor resulting from his individual features. These superlative and prime examples could be "one-of-a-kind." One can guess that the mayor is on the far right; the owner of the mill (with pipe in hand) is next to him; the elderly man in blue/white striped shirt could be a farmer, etc. The farmer who is driving the wagon has his knees bent enambling him to sit on the wagon that hauls the flour sacks stamped "M. St." (Margarete Steiff). All with old printed button. Courtesy John R. Fazendin.

The Blacksmith's Shop, (4½ ft. high), contains all the tools of the trade: Fire blower, forge, hammers and anvil. These toys on show, originating from the 1933 Chicago World's Fair, dealt with a theme inspired by every-day German village life with the inhabitants engaged in their respective endeavors. One can clearly visualize the blacksmith (wearing a leather apron) prepare to shoe a horse. Note, the costumes are accurate in every detail. Descriptions of some people and animals follow.

Mechanical dolls from the German Village: 16"/41 cm. caricatures; all with typical center seam in the felt construction; all with old printed button and in pristine condition. The original shoes as well as the accessories are available but not present in the photograph. These gadgets, for example a fishing pole, provide an integral part of the scene because they enable the automated doll to perform its assigned activity. Note the glass eyes with a black dot for pupil seen on some of the faces with excessive caricature. Left to right: Blacksmith holding a hammer with his right hand moving up and down; a woman beating the grain with a stick held in her hand; a woman shaking out the checkered rug; man with stick in hand also beating the grain; the fifth figure is a fisherman holding a fishing pole; the last figure is another farmer holding a stick and beating the grain. These timeless mechanical dolls hold great fascination for the advanced collector. Courtesy John R. Fazendin.

Horses from the German Village: 20"/51 cm. high, 23"/58 cm. long; felt over a steel frame; straw stuffed; glass eyes. Note the elaborate leather pulling harnesses of the type used on draft horses. The animals are beautifully sculpted with utmost fidelity to Margarete Steiff's craftsmanship. Rare large size, ca. 1920s. All with old printed button. Courtesy John R. Fazendin.

"Bully" dog as a policeman directing traffic: 17"/43 cm., mechanical; left arm goes out straight and finger points to channel the traffic; the right arm moves to stop the traffic. Of the many Steiff renditions of "Bully", this large example shows the most originality. Note the meticulous detail of his uniform. Old printed button. Courtesy John R. Fazendin.

Nuances of comedy are seen in the group of humanized dressed ducks, 13″/33 cm. to 15″/38 cm. They are non-mechanical but do not need automation to make their statement. Note the successful combination of mohair and felt, and the original cane that one of the ducks carries. When considering a value, one must consider the possibility that they could never be replaced. All with old printed button. Courtesy John R. Fazendin.

The fox as Bandleader is non-mechanical: 20″/51 cm. tall, mohair and felt, glass eyes; note that the design of the right hand enables him to hold the original baton. The original shoes were missing when the photograph was made but are available. The large Teddy Bear is mechanical: 20″/51 cm. tall; he raises his hand to his head as though to remove a hat. A most impressive figure of a performing bear. Small fox on right is mechanical: 10″/25 cm. tall; the legs move in a swinging motion while he remains seated. The two largest figures in the "Animal Village" are the splendid Bandleader and the dressed bear. All with old printed button. Courtesy John R. Fazendin.

Humanized chicken and roosters: 15″/38 cm. tall; mohair and felt. The center rooster is the vocalist with a mechanical beak that opens and closes. The aesthetic accompanists are: Left, non-mechanical rooster holding his original guitar; hen on right (also non-mechanical) holding her original banjo. Note how effective the simple and colorful clothes are. All with old printed button. Courtesy John R. Fazendin.

Boxers fittingly portrayed with the head of "Bully." Both are 17″/43 cm. tall. The dog on left is mechanized to move his arms for body blows. His bulging eyes are green glass with a black pupil glancing to the side. The center "Bully" is non-mechanical with adjustable arms bent at the elbow. He gives upper cuts to the head, and his legs are in a crouched, fighting position. His large eyes are orange glass. The dressed dog on the right appears to be the trainer and is non-mechanical, 13″/33 cm. tall. All with old printed button. Courtesy John R. Fazendin.

Mechanical performing animals that are humanized: Dogs from the gym, 12″/30.5 cm. to 14″/36 cm. tall. Left, mechanical moving from the waist, he exercises by touching his toes; fourth and fifth from the left are also mechanical and do the same exercise. The three dogs in center are mechanical and move their legs while bending their knees. Some of the dogs are tired from exercising and have their tongues hanging out. A marvelous group. All with old printed button. Provenance increases value. Courtesy John R. Fazendin.

Trio of mechanical elephants that move their limbs individually "in time with the music." Grey mohair, 16″/41 cm. high; straw stuffed; fully jointed; shoe button eyes. A non-mechanical fully jointed elephant is shown in the 1907 catalog and continued in production, true to the original design, until the 1920s. The exact dating of these charming models is of no consequence. They are so very rare and desirable today. Note the boxer trunks on the center elephant, adding further humor. All with old printed button. Courtesy John R. Fazendin.

From the Village: Pigs, 13″/33 cm. high, light gold mohair (Teddy Bear color); straw stuffed; fully jointed with knees bent to sit in the sporting arena; bright blue glass eyes, velveteen noses with painted markings. Pigs as spectators are truly unique. Old printed button. Teddy Bear, 10″/24 cm. off-white (desirable color) mohair, straw stuffed, f.j., small glass eyes; brown hard cotton twisted floss nose/mouth and four claws; heavy weight felt pads; perfectly curved paws and long thin feet. Early printed button and remnants of the 1926-1934 *red* ID. tag dating him 1932-1933 (the year we know he graced the display in Chicago). Note the quality detailing of such a small Teddy Bear. Courtesy John R. Fazendin.

Animal dolls: Animals costumed as humans are considered "dolls." The first animal dolls made by Steiff date from 1897. This appealing quartet of fully jointed mohair rabbits are 9"/23 cm. to 13"/33 cm. tall. The second from the left is mechanized to move both arms. Note the high coloring on the male rabbit. The rabbit is a favorite vehicle for costuming. All with old printed button. Courtesy John R. Fazendin.

Small monkeys from the "Animal Village" shown at the 1933 Chicago World's Fair. All are mechanical in the top row: Left, plays the mouth organ; center chimpanzee plays a violin; right plays an accordian. The original instruments are available but not present in the photograph. The monkey on chair is non-mechanical and was never treasured as the others who were carefully stored conserving their original condition. He has been enjoyed on a shelf these many years. There is some damage to his felt hands which can be easily restored. All with old printed button. Courtesy John R. Fazendin.

XII. Costumed Animals

Ned the well dressed Ted: 7½″/19 cm., gold mohair head and mitts, muslin body; hard stuffed cotton, jointed by bendable wire; shoe button eyes/white felt backing; black floss nose and double stitched mouth; spiffy in his blue felt pants and shoes, beige vest and light blue jacket. Because of the doll-like quality, dressed aniamls are great favorites among collectors. Possible Schuco, ca. 1940. Courtesy Kathy Teske.

A treasure; pair of dressed Steiff foxes: 9″/23 cm. tall, No. 325, raised script ear button, "Made in U.S. Zone Germany" tag; mohair head, hands and feet; body, arms and legs are cloth; jointed heads only; squeakers. Ethnic costume of felt hats/feather, felt and cotton outfits. Steiff collectors love the dressed animals and these two are a prime example of why the demand remains high. Add value for a matched pair. Courtesy Jane L. Viprino.

1983 Teddy Roosevelt commemorative Limited Edition set to celebrate the 125th birthday of the President. No. 0210,22, 8½"/22 cm., brass, beige and white mohair bears reflecting the theme of the famous hunting expedition. Made in an issue of 10,000 and not a good seller. Some objected to a *cardboard* fire; others to the use of leatherette instead of leather boots; environmentalists to the sport of hunting. Half of the sets were broken up and the desirable size of bears were sold unboxed, undressed and retagged without a catalogue number for $55.00 each. The price on the remaining 5,000 nimrod (hunter) sets could esculate slowly. (Author).

Matched pair of dressed rabbits: 9"/23 cm. tall, raised script ear button and "Made in US Zone Germany" tag; cloth body, arms and legs; short pile synthetic plush head, ears, hands and feet; jointed head only; cloth outfits. Note: Demand is high for all animals tagged, "US Zone, Germany." Courtesy Jane L. Viprino.

The original huntsmen/rifles were dressed by Theodore Roosevelt's caterer to be used as table decorations for Alice's wedding. The above hunter (one of a set) was issued in 1953, the year commemorating 50 years of Steiff Teddies. Size: 8½"/22 cm., No. 5322 N, snow-white thick pile mohair, straw stuffed, f.j., glass eyes, dark brown twisted floss nose/mouth and claws; felt clothing; boots are leather. Courtesy Robin Lowe.

Gund, 17″/43 cm., snow white rayon plush, straw stuffed, un-jointed; pink glass eyes, floss nose/mouth, felt mitten hands and shoes/cardboard innersoles; all decked out in her Easter finery, ca. early 1950s. Increase value for original box. Typical of Gund's high quality continuing today. Courtesy Kay Bransky.

"Nikili," 13½″/46 cm., No. 91/36/736, raised script button: Mohair, jointed head and arms, glass eyes, open mouth; felt tie, cummerbund and shoes; cotton skirt. She was also made in a 10″/25 cm. size. Rare and desirable early dressed rabbit, ca. 1958. Courtesy Dee Hockenberry.

Building blocks in the evolution of mid-20th century stuffed toys: Schuco, 13″/33 cm. Yes/No "Tricky" monkey with lever exposed; luxurious brown mohair and felt, f.j., ca. 1950s. Gund tagged Bellhop, 18″/46 cm., vinyl painted face, open/close eyes with eyelashes, red twill outfit (metal buttons, gripper snaps), felt trim; black cloth stuffed body, black curly cotton plush hair and arms. Note the beautifully modelled hands only achieved with vinyl (and bisque), ca. early 1960s. Right: 18″/46 cm., Merrythought comical bellhop monkey; a Lawson Wood design, ca. 1950s, un-jointed brown rayon plush body and head, felt ears, hands and feet, painted and molded velvet face, felt jacket/cap. Special. Courtesy Ellyn McCorkell.

Army Mule and Navy Goat: 6½"/16 cm., high, 6"/15 cm. long, tan cotton plush, straw stuffed, unjointed. Army has amber glass eyes, cotton mane and felt tail. Navy has brown/black glass googly eyes and felt horns. From original owner, ca. late 1940s. Compo doll, 30"/76 cm., flange neck, stuffed body/limbs. Purported to be Red Grange, ca. 1920s. Marked "Sterling Doll Co." All courtesy Ellyn McCorkell.

"Ossili" rabbit in felt gardening clothes: 12"/30 cm., No. 7800/30, white mohair with light brown markings, straw stuffed, jointed head and arms, plastic eyes, pink floss nose and open felt mouth; brown suede-like foot pads; raised script button and old C.T., ca. late 1960s-early 1970s. Desirable. Courtesy Dee Hockenberry.

"Country Mouse" House with Steiff mouse: Marketed in the 1960s, the wooden house (stamped "Made in Western Germany") has swing out doors, a mirror and a bench. Missing are the dishes, pans, cleaning materials, quilt and ladder. Rare if complete. Mouse with gingham apron, No. 4308,40. Her friends are: 3¼"/08 cm., No. 2174/08; grey and white mohair with felt hands, feet and tail, straw stuffed, plastic eyes, glass bead nose. The grey mouse is the rarest. F.A.O. Schwarz is noted for "equipping" an animal. Courtesy Kirk Stines.

Steiff animals dressed by F.A.O. Schwarz: "Pieps" was introduced in 1958 and remained in production until 1978. This dressed model available 1967-1970: 3½"/08 cm., No. 4308,04 (see description with Mouse House); dressed in cotton clown suit by F.A.O. Schwarz who also dressed a Bride, Groom, Ballerina, "Queen of the Ball," Senorita, Hawaiian Mouse, and "Princess Royal" Mouse. Any of these are *rare* today. Baby Bear of The Three Bears: 7"/17.5 cm., "Original Teddy," mohair with shaved nose, straw stuffed, f.j., plastic eyes, floss nose/mouth, Trevira velvet pads, ca. late 1960s. Bears used for this set in the middle '60s were "long-fur-on-the-nose" variety; then came the shaved nose with felt pads and finally these with shaved nose and Trevira velvet pads. Extremely rare. Courtesy Kirk Stines.

Rainbow of colors: 1960s (2½"/6.3 cm.) and 1970s (3½"/9 cm.), mohair on the patented metal frame, metal push-pin eyes, thread nose/mouth, f.j.; colors catalogued as chocolate brown, pale gold (red nose/mouth), medium tan, deep gold and brownish tan. The center pair was dressed as a special edition for the Enchanted Doll House and featured in their 1970s catalogue. These and the jointed panda (made 1930-1960) command the highest prices. Beware: Tiny German handmade bears (2½"/6.3 cm.) strikingly similar to Schuco are new on the market for $12.00. Courtesy Wanda Loukides.

"Rico," humanized rabbit, 17"/43 cm., No. 7828/43; white mohair head, tail and feet; sewn-to-body red Dralon ski togs, removable blue felt scarf and hat (often lost); cardboard lined ears; f.j. with a doll-like quality; blue and black plastic eyes; pink twisted floss nose, pink felt open mouth with black painted outline; teardrop-shape pads on feet only; nylon whiskers. Desirable, ca. 1974. (Author)

XIII. Steiff Animals Before 1940

"Fluffy" *katze* (ca. 1928) comes with a true story. In 1985 she was found to have a Steiff button in each (unmatched) ear, one of which was a dog's ear. Returning from a trip in 1928-1929, the father of Joan and Sydney Robinson brought each daughter a Steiff toy; "Fluffy" cat and "Molly" dog. In the dim past, the former lost an ear. The girls' enterprising mother quickly replaced it with one from Sydney's "loved to death" dog. When Sydney recently announced that she had become a Teddy Bear collector, Joan gave the virtually unplayed with "Fluffy" to her sister. Now cleaned and restored with a proper new cat's ear she sits with pride. "Fluffy's" two ear buttons proved more unique than just an error on Steiff's part. "Fluffy" was made in 7 sizes for at least 10 years; a good seller and now so rare. 10″/25 cm. tall; grey and white mohair 1″ long; elegant large glass eyes with the iris handpainted in 2 shades of bluish green; pink twisted floss nose and red floss claws; squeaker. The girls called these furry pets after the names on the chest tags at that time. Courtesy Sydney Robinson Charles.

Puss 'N Boots, ca. 1910: 11½″/29 cm., grey long pile mohair, *horsehair* stuffed, wood disc jointed head, arms, legs and *tail*, green glass eyes, rust color braided floss nose, mouth and claws, grey felt ears and pads; green velvet boots (worn) with gold braid. Note the long arms as found on Teddy Bears of this period. Extraordinary early cat. Courtesy Christine Irr.

A real "porker": 14″/35.5 cm., pinkish blonde thick mohair, straw stuffed, swivel head with cloth pad at neck joint, arms jointed by bendable wire, replaced glass eyes; dark pink velveteen nose, ear linings and hands/stitched fingers; pink velveteen half-open mouth and foot pads with cardboard innersoles; wire in tail to curl. Maker unknown, ca. 1920-1930. Courtesy Christine Irr.

The unique design and sense of fun adds value to the monkey: 23½"/60 cm., straw stuffed; unjointed; felt/flannel molded mask face, painted side glancing eyes, red mouth and nostrils; two silly tiny ears; removable white collar bound in red cotton; red flannel sewn-to-body shirt, black trousers and beige tail are bound with red cotton; backs of hands and head are woven *horsehair* (similar to early buggy robes); gravity-type voice box. Commercially made, possible English, ca. 1900. Bear on cast iron wheels, 11½"/29 cm. high, brown mohair, ca. pre-1920. (Author).

Victorian Poodle: 12"/30.5 cm. high, 13"/33 cm. long, straw stuffed, unjointed, white flannel body with angora fur mane; brown glass eyes, black floss nose/mouth. This type of flannel toy is usually found in smaller sizes. Maker unknown, ca. 1910. Courtesy Dot Franklin.

Terrier, left: 12"/30.5 cm. long, blonde mohair; straw stuffed, swivel head, wire armature supports legs; brown glass eyes, black floss nose and mouth, no claws, longish feet, black felt lined ears sewn down. Unknown maker, ca. 1950. Spaniel, 15"/38 cm. long, light gold long pile mohair, all straw stuffed, f.j., black shoe button eyes deeply set, dark brown twisted floss nose and wide mouth, 3 claws; long floppy ears and beaver-like tail. Unknown maker, ca. 1920. Worn. Note: The fur falls out of many non-bear early animals. Compared to the Teddy Bears of the same period, the (dog's) mohair is a poor grade with fewer threads per square inch in the backing. (Author).

Steiff Yes/No baby Orangutan, ca. 1930s: 8½″/22 cm., burnished gold long pile mohair, straw stuffed, f.j., glass eyes inset into felt face/painted features; felt hands and feet with stitched fingers. Original rayon bow *sewn* to chest. This appears to be the largest size Steiff made of this mechanical monkey. From 1930-1950, differentiating some Steiff from Schuco becomes difficult. Steiff made animals with a Yes/No mechanism; for example, a 1955 Teddy (8″/20 cm.) and a chimpanzee. Moreover there is an old Steiff dwarf with metal spectacles and a mohair hat with the Yes/No function; a Steiff postman with a Schuco mechanism including a marked "Schuco" key. However, this confusion does not alter value. (Author).

Pre-1930s rabbit: 7″/17.5 cm. tall (inc. ears), orange and white mohair; straw stuffed; jointed head only; glass eyes, black twisted floss nose/mouth; no squeaker. Printed Steiff button "ff" underscored. Mohair in this rare orange color is also seen on a dressed rabbit in the Fazendin Collection. The Steiff Co. is justly proud of the wonderful rabbits they have manufactured for many years. Courtesy Kelly Tidwell.

F.W. Woodnough, Inc. made the unforgettable "Honey Boy," ca. 1930: 8″/20 cm., jointed head only, a replica of a real (bruin-type) bear; black long pile mohair, white mohair "V" shape inset on chest; low set small ears, open velvet-lined mouth; stubby tail. The years have left him with only one glass eye; fortunately he can tilt his head to see more. The Woodnough designs are highly original for their time. Extremely rare. Courtesy Carolyn Dockray.

"Jack," Airdale: 6"/15 cm. high, mohair, straw stuffed, unjointed; glass eyes, floss nose/mouth, *working* squeaker which is in itself unusual; some bare patches but a lovable expression. Any pre-WW II Steiff animal is rare; without positive I.D., this example could be overlooked; old printed button "ff" underscored and remnants of red (faded to orange) I.D. tag date toy 1926-1934. Courtesy Kirk Stines.

Paper chest tag: Bear with a "watermelon" (smiling) mouth used from 1927-1950. Note the split metal grommet to reinforce the hole in the somewhat heavier weight cardboard. This chest tag is found combined with the pewter color printed button "ff" underscored that dates further back in time (1905).

Steiff wool "Pom-Pom" bird: 2½"/6.3 cm., wool, felt beak and tail, glass eyes, wire feet; attached by old printed button "ff" underscored is the *red* I.D. tag reading, "*geschutzt*" (protected by law or copyright), "Made in Germany," on one side; on reverse, "6508 Steiff Original," ca. 1926-1934. During this time Steiff made more than a dozen different wool (yarn) pom-pom animals. These are rare today because they were easily misplaced and never treasured. Courtesy Kirk Stines.

"Bully," 10″/25 cm., No. 3325,2, stamped on red paper I.D. tag (used 1926-1934); large pewter ear button "ff" underscored, cream color short pile mohair with inset rust color mohair markings, velveteen snout/airbrushed markings; straw stuffed, jointed head only; large orange glass eyes; dark brown silky twisted floss nose in life-like style; horsehair ruff on bias tape; "Bully Steiff Original" on 1½″/3.8 cm. metal rimmed tag with large attached brass bell; note the contoured haunches and long feet with 3 floss claws. "Mopsy," 5″/12.5 cm., No. 4010/12, shaded beige mohair (59% wool, 41% cotton), googly black/white eyes, black floss nose, red felt tongue (*felt* tongues on Steiff animals are considered undesirable); right ear stitched down. A long production life and one of the last mohair animals to be discontinued. Cute but common. (Author).

Steiff kangaroo, ca. 1930s, printed button "ff" underscored: 13½″/34 cm., all-over tan mohair, straw stuffed, jointed head and arms; glass eyes, twisted floss nose/mouth and claws. Mohair baby as above; short front legs, long hind legs. The precursor of the 1950s more highly colored mohair kangaroo. In 1975 "Linda" kangaroo was once again available; this time in a fur imitation. Courtesy Robin Lowe.

Skye Terrier: 5½″/14 cm. high, 9″/23 cm. long; old printed Steiff button "ff" underscored; old C.T. (square bear head/watermelon mouth); long pile silky mohair; mint condition from 1930. Rare. Courtesy Jane L. Viprino.

Left, Terrier with Grisly I.D. (metal shield imbedded in left shoulder): 8½"/22 cm. long, golden mohair with black and brown markings, straw stuffed, unjointed, glass eyes. Note the similarity to Steiff's Airedale "Terry," however, the nose is stitched with a *coarser* twisted floss and there are no claws, ca. early 1960s. Right, 11½"/28 cm. long, mohair with residual markings, straw stuffed, unjointed; fine *yarn* stitched nose/mouth, glass eyes. Unknown maker. Scotties, Spaniels and Terriers abounded, ca. 1930s. Courtesy Gaye N. Delling.

Steiff felt pony: 10½"/27 cm. high, 11"/28 cm. long, *all felt* with painted "dappling effect," straw stuffed, unjointed, glass eyes. This beautiful model was also made on wooden wheels, ca. 1937. Mint. Horses are one of Steiff's most unsuccessful animals. In a live horse the muscle caricature is all important. These skin folds are difficult to copy in a stuffed toy. Courtesy Robin Lowe.

Zebra, 10"/25 cm. high. 13"/33 cm. long, cotton plush/airbrushed markings, nicely contoured straw stuffed legs, hard cotton stuffed body, unjointed; clear glass eyes, black twisted floss nose; black mohair mane and tail trim. Answers to name of "Theodotius," from author's childhood, 1938 exactly. Well-made (probable) American.

White rabbit: 5½"/14 cm., straw stuffed, jointed head only, *over-size rimmed glass eyes*, pink floss nose/black floss outline, printed Steiff button "ff" underscored. Note the long skinny feet on this 1930s model. Courtesy Rosemary Moran.

Beloved cat, 9½"/24 cm., luxurious gold mohair as found on Teddy Bears, f.j., straw stuffed; the arms, legs and head are *hard*, the body is softer because of wear on the squeaker. Green glass stickpin eyes, rust color floss nose/mouth and claws, *horsehair* whiskers, felt pads/cardboard innersoles, stiff tail that curls. Body and head are broad and flat. Courtesy Kelly Tidwell.

XIV. Steiff Animals, 1940 - Present
Steiff Cats

KERSA cat: 12″/30.5 cm., black mohair, straw stuffed, f.j., green and black large glass eyes, small red floss nose/mouth; white whiskers; tan felt hand pads; red felt boots. Metal tag on foot, "KERSA/Made in Germany," ca. 1940. Rare example of Puss 'N Boots. Courtesy Dee Hockenberry.

Gund cat, 16″/41 cm., white synthetic plush, unjointed, soft stuffed, painted cotton molded face with green eyes and painted wiskers. Original 1950s rayon bow. Interesting. Courtesy Ellyn McCorkell.

Unmistakable charm of early toys: Left: Kitty, 4½″/11 cm. high, 6½″/16 cm. long, high quality composition, ca. 1930, jointed only head and back legs (posable), painted facial features with green eyes. Red celluloid Teddy Bear, 4″/10 cm., elastic jointing of arms and legs only, painted features including detail of pads and claws. Also available are elephants, tigers etc.; often bought for Christmas tree decorations, ca. 1930s. Right: Rattle head cat, 5½″/14 cm., unjointed, cotton hard stuffed, polka dot cotton, painted celluloid head stitched to body through holes, ears inset through holes. In back seam, a seldom seen tag, "Krueger, Rattle Head Family," ca. 1930. Courtesy Susan Roeder.

"Lizzy" cat: 8½"/22 cm., No. 2716/22, standing with tail straight up; white and orange Dralon inset markings; green plastic eyes, pink twisted floss nose/mouth; cute cat with a distinctive expression; raised script ear button, ca. late 1960s. Also made in a 6"/15 cm. size; additionally, there was a "Lizzy" made in the preferred mohair. Courtesy Chris McWilliams.

"Cattie," 9"/23 cm., No. 2770/23: Sitting; tabby striped 80% Dralon, 20% cotton; green plastic eyes; pink twisted floss nose /mouth; nylon filament whiskers; also made in a smaller 7"/18 cm. size. At the same time, ca. 1973, there was a mohair sitting cat named "Susi" Courtesy Chris McWilliams.

"Fiffy," cat, lying: 10"/24 cm. long, No. 2325,1; Tabby striped mohair, see the plain center band on back found only on Steiff Tabbies (all varieties); soft stuffed swivel head; green glass eyes; rose twisted floss nose/mouth and claws. Note the mohair is clipped on face and at ear tips; a time consuming but effective detail. Companionable and desirable pet, ca. late 1950s. (Author).

Puss 'N Boots made by Grisly: 11″/28 cm., high quality black and white mohair, jointed head and arms only, plastic eyes, pink floss nose/mouth; red plastic boots and felt tie. In 1974 the Grisly logo on a metal shield imbedded in chest was replaced by this paper tag, ca. 1980s. Gebr. Hermann black cat, 4½″/12 cm., 53% wool, 47% cotton, (mohair) unjointed, green plastic eyes, pink floss nose and mouth. See pg. 36 of Gebr. Hermann KG 1970s catalogue. Courtesy Chris McWilliams.

Gebrueder Hermann KG Catalog, ca. 1970s

Mohair kitties of unknown origin; nevertheless a good find for the many cat collectors. All are 4½″/11.5 cm. high; left and right have *sliced in* ears and embroidered noses; kitty sitting right has a swivel head; center has embroidered mouth and *heart-shape plastic* nose. Courtesy Chris McWilliams.

Steiff "Tom Cat"; 5½″/14 cm. high, No. 2860/14, black mohair, green plastic eyes, stitched nose. Also made in a 8½″/22 cm. size as well as 4″/10 cm. in velvet. A fanciful representation of the ubiquitous black cat; fun for Halloween; incised script button, ca. 1960-1970. Common. Boxer: 6½″/17 cm., No. 4100/17 high mohair, plastic eyes, twisted floss nose/mouth and 3 claws; face flaps of black velveteen; original blue leather collar; raised script button, ca. 1960s. Also made in a 4″/10 cm. size. Somewhat hard to find. Courtesy Chris McWilliams.

A bevy of mohair cats, ca. 1930-1970. The most noteworthy of this company are "Snurry," sleeping, top row, 3rd from left; bottom row, "Gussy," white mohair/black markings, 4th from left; "Kitty Cat," fully jointed tabby, far right. Cats (kittys) are extremely *personal* pets. A stuffed toy cannot look like the person's *particular cat*. Dog lovers are less finicky. Courtesy Susan Roeder.

159

Steiff Dogs

Knickerbocker tagged dog: 13″/33 cm. long; short white wool plush; straw stuffed, jointed head only, brown felt nose, floss mouth, no claws; black metal eyes, brown cotton plush ears. One of the fine quality Terriers made by various manufacturers, ca. 1940. Courtesy Ellyn McCorkell.

Made in Japan: 5½″/14 cm., burnt orange velveteen, straw stuffed, unjointed, hunter green velveteen ears sewn on, black *yarn* nose/mouth, yellow glass eyes; blue rayon seam binding as bow/old brass bell; has its own 1930s charm. Courtesy Gaye N. Delling.

Scotty: 5½″/14 cm. high, No. 1314; thick black mohair; straw stuffed, swivel head; unusual glassine eyes that are "people shape"; black floss nose; leather collar with bell; raised script button, C.T. printed "Scotty," one of 4 sizes made a short time, ca. 1950s. Rare. Courtesy Chris McWilliams.

Spaniel nightdress case: 21″/53 cm., long pile white mohair with inset black mohair markings, unjointed; brown glass eyes, black twisted floss nose/mouth, 3 floss claws; white rayon satin quilted lining; zippered. ''Merrythought'' tag is machine-stitched to rear underside; made 1950-1959. English Sheep Dog, 13″/33 cm. high, 14″/36 cm. long, white curly long pile mohair with grey mohair inset markings; straw and kapok stuffed (wires contour legs); jointed head only, clear glass eyes, black twisted floss nose with downward curve (often seen on Merrythought toys); 3 claws, also found on Merrythought (and other) animals; a hard-to-find example for a dog collection, ca. 1950. Courtesy Carol Rockwell.

''Laika'' (Spacedog) Husky: 6½″/17 cm., No. 1317,0, white mohair airbrushed in golds, almond (human) shaped glass eyes, twisted floss nose/mouth; 10½″/27 cm. size also shown in 1958 New Model Catalog. Raised script button. Rare. Courtesy Jane L. Viprino.

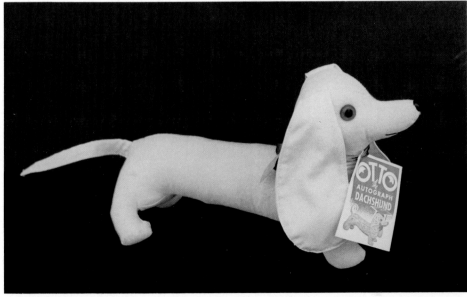

Autograph dog, ''Otto,'' ca. 1941: 11″/28 cm. long, off white closely woven canvas tightly stuffed with cotton to provide the perfect surface for a permanent ink record of names and quotes. The dachshund has glass eyes, black plastic nose and mouth stitched with button thread. Tagged ''Collegiate Manufacturing Co., Ames, Iowa.'' Autograph Teddy Bears were also available. Rare to find an unused example. (Author).

"Beppo," Dachshund: 6½"/17 cm., No. 5317; brown and tan mohair; straw stuffed; f.j.; glass eyes; twisted floss nose (downward points); felt tongue in open mouth; floss claws; original red leather collar. This scarce dog, ca. 1950s, is found on "want lists." He was followed by "Lumpi," unjointed legs, in the 1960s. Courtesy Dee Hockenberry.

White Scotty: 8½"/22 cm. high, No. 1322,02, snow white long pile mohair, straw stuffed, jointed head only. Raised script ear button; "Made in US Zone Germany" tag. Steiff listed this dog as a "Sealyham" but dog experts would recognize this breed as a West Highland White Terrier or "Westie." Catalogued in 4 sizes. In 1948 it was not a good seller because of soiling. Rare. Courtesy Jane L. Viprino.

Chow listed as Pomeranian in the 1957 catalogue: 4"/10 cm., No. 69/3510, sitting position as if he could speak; white wool plush, straw stuffed, white velveteen muzzle and ears, black floss nose/mouth; brown glass eyes with a painted *red* highlight; unjointed; one size only. *Rare.* Courtesy Chris McWilliams.

"Bazi," Dachshund: 4"/10 cm., No. 1310, mohair, straw stuffed, swivel head, glass eyes, floss nose, blue leather collar and bell; raised script button; note the subtle touches to give expression. This puppy also came in a sitting model as well as on wooden wheels. Owner's only Steiff animal from childhood, ca. 1958. Courtesy Kirk Stines.

"Cockie," small: 4"/10 cm., No. 1310,00, reddish brown mohair, straw stuffed, jointed head only, glass eyes, open velvet mouth; three sizes were made, 4"/10 cm., 6½"/18 cm. and 10"/28 cm. This model was replaced after 1957 with a brown/white spotted (closed mouth) Cocker Spaniel. Note the puppy-like expression. Hard to find. Courtesy Jane L. Viprino.

Collie: 7"/25 cm. high, reclining, No. 4250/25; long and short pile mohair with life-like markings in golds and charcoal; straw and cotton stuffed; brown glass eyes; black twisted floss nose; red felt tongue in open felt mouth outlined in black/teeth; 3 floss claws; painted mohair pads. Reclining animals were not introduced into the Steiff line until the 1950s. Note this thick coated herding dog of Scotland would combine well with the flowing lines of *art nouveau* decor. Desirable, ca. 1960s. Courtesy Marianne Gardner.

"Revue Susi," 11″/28 cm. high, No. 3328,03; long and short blonde mohair airbrushed in golds, straw stuffed, jointed head, black/white googly glass eyes, black twisted floss nose/(downward points), mouth and claws; squeaker; original collar and old C.T., ca. 1960-1970. Common dog but hard to find in this largest of 4 sizes. Courtesy Dee Hockenberry.

A delightful mascot pet of the Margarete Steiff Co., "Cockie,' the inquisitive black and white Spaniel: 7½″/19 cm. high, 8″/20 cm. long, No. 4276/19; mohair (51% wool, 49% cotton); straw stuffed, swivel head; plastic eyes; floss nose/painted mouth; original red leatherette collar, ca. 1960s. Popular. Courtesy Rosemary Moran.

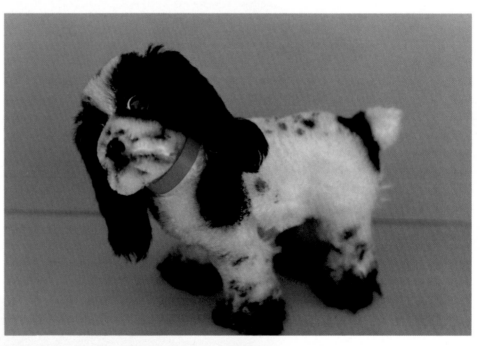

There is a large spectrum of dogs available for the many dog lovers. Left: 7″/18 cm. high, white *cotton* plush Terrier; unjointed, cotton stuffed; shoe button-type eyes; bakelite nose, floss mouth, ca. 1950. Spaniel: 4″/10 cm. high, straw stuffed; synthetic plush with short nap; glass eyes. The ears are *sliced into* the head and the nose is stitched with *thread;* indicative of Japanese manufacture, ca. 1950. No real collectibility. Steiff "Dalmation," 6½″/17 cm. high, No. 4060/17; white mohair spotted black; swivel head; glass eyes, floss nose and 3 claws; open velvet mouth. Also came in 4″/10 cm. size, ca. 1960s. Hard to find. Courtesy Ellyn McCorkell.

"Corso," Afghan: 13½"/35 cm., No. 2335,00, apricot colored long pile mohair (not the typical "gold" color of many Steiffs such as the "Revue Susi" Cocker and several bears); straw stuffed, lying posture, glass eyes. An 8½"/22 cm. size also made, ca. 1960. Rare hound. Courtesy Jane L. Viprino.

Character dog, 10"/25 cm. high, 10"/25 cm. long, mohair/inset colors, eyes housed under a celluloid-type bubble, open red felt mouth, velvet-lined ears, hard-rubber molded nose. Bought in Germany, ca. 1960; possible Schuco similar to their "Tramp" model. Nodder, 13"/33 cm., papier mache "Bobby," marked "Made in Scotland." Courtesy Beverly Krein.

J.K. Farnell dog: 7"/17.5 cm. long, white mohair, straw stuffed, unjointed, glass eyes, floss nose/mouth. Tagged on stomach, "Farnell Alpha Hygienic Soft Toy Made in England." Tag increases value. Good condition. Courtesy Dee Hockenberry.

"Bernie Samarit," 7″/18 cm. high, 9″/23 cm. long, No. 1322,09, raised script button, old C.T. in German language. Off-white mohair airbrushed with shades of brown, unjointed, straw stuffed, black twisted floss nose, mouth is airbrushed, tan plastic eyes, biggish feet with 3 floss claws (on dogs Steiff often used 3 claws not the 4 found on Teddy Bears); barking squeaker and original wooden keg. Note the bushy tail that is straw stuffed and curled at tip. Rare, ca. 1964. Mint. Courtesy Bill Gardner.

Electrola Fox Terrier, "His Master's Voice" (R.C.A.): 5″/12 cm., No. 4420/12, white sheared plush, brown mohair ears, plastic eyes, twisted floss nose/mouth; original collar. Issued as a "Novelty" in 1968, the smallest of three sizes. The large sizes were discontinued by 1970. Hard to find, as are many animals from this period. Raised script button. Courtesy Dee Hockenbery.

Large "Foxy": Standing Foxterrier, 11"/28 cm. high, white silky mohair with brown and charcoal markings; straw stuffed, unjointed; glass eyes; black twisted floss nose (downward points), mouth and claws; side push working squeaker, ca. late 1950s; the second largest of 6 sizes. The smaller sizes are common. Mint. Courtesy Dee Hockenberry.

"Biggie," Beagle dog: 4"/10 cm., No. 4090/10; miniature from 1972 with original price tag, $7.50. White mohair with shades of brown and black; swivel head; brown plastic eyes; black stitched nose with red stitched tongue; the same body design is used on other sitting dogs. Courtesy Marge Vance.

Hermann Poodle (silver tag): 9"/23 cm. high, 8"/20 cm. long, straw stuffed, f.j., white long and short pile mohair; glass eyes with white "eyedot"; hard plastic nose; red felt tongue; squeaker; missing collar, ca. 1970. Courtesy Kay Bransky.

"Waldi," Dachshund: Left, 13″/33 cm. long, copper color long curly mohair, straw stuffed, unjointed; black plastic eyes; black floss nose, painted mouth and claws; original *blue bow*, ca. 1950s-1970s. Note that the Gebr. Hermann KG long mohair Dachshund has a *collar*. See pg. 34 of 1970s catalogue. Right, 11″/28 cm. long, copper color mohair mellowed to pink; the short legs have collapsed, but the facial markings remain true. No I.D. An exercise in comparing mint to less than mint. Common. Courtesy Rosemary Moran.

Gebrueder Hermann KG. Catalog ca. 1970s.

Rabbits and Domestic Animals

Miniature velvet pigs (this size came *without* chest tags): Left, 3″/7.5 cm., No. 1407, Or, pink velvet, straw stuffed, glass eyes, felt nose, vinyl covered rope tail. Made early 1950s to 1965; in 1970 the model was made of synthetic. Right, 3″/7.5 cm., Wild boar baby, brown velvet with fine markings, straw stuffed, plastic eyes, felt nose, rope tail, ca. 1965-1971. Made with glass eyes from '50s to '60s. Courtesy Kirk Stines.

"Uncle Jacques," a friendly rabbit: 22″/56 cm., grey and white thick synthetic plush, stuffed with shredded clippings, f.j., yellow plastic eyes, brown ultra suede nose, ear linings, pads and removable bag containing felt carrots; heavy duty nylon whiskers. From Dakin's "Elegante" series identified by leather tag. Carefully handcrafted from the finest materials, he is destined to be a classic. In 1984 retail price, $60.00. (Author).

Impressive collection of barnyard animals showing the range of Steiff: Super Molly calf, 40″/99 cm., No. 0365/99; pair of Calves lying, No. 3795/27; Cosy Flora calf twins, standing, No. 5477/25; Rico horse No. 3760/25; Molly pig, 19½″/45 cm., No. 0360/45; Cosy Pig twins, No. 5415/28; Cosy Piggy triplets, standing, No. 5414/18; all are woven fur, surface washable. Courtesy Beth Savino, Hobby Center Toys.

"Knickerbocker Kuddles Bunny," 13"/33 cm. tall, long pile white mohair, straw stuffed head, soft body, unjointed, glass eyes, stitched and painted nose/mouth. Originally sold as an infant toy; because of the high quality, it has collector appeal. Note the expression and floppy ears, ca. 1955-1960. Courtesy Kay Bransky.

"Begging Rabbit" as Harvey admiring himself: 20"/50 cm. (without ears), brown/white mohair, swivel head, jointed arms, white mohair airbrushed in browns, felt ear linings touched with pink, pink floss nose and closed mouth; tail. Courtesy Diane Hoffman.

Easter might be considered second only to Christmas as an inspiration for stuffed toys. Left: "Niki" translated from *Karnickel*, a bunny rabbit. Steiff's early paints were fugitive and have faded to an over all cream color mohair: 11½"/28 cm., No. 5328,2; straw stuffed, f.j.; glass eyes, pink floss nose, open felt mouth; felt pads on extra long feet. "Niki" was reissued in 1985. He has always been more desirable than the similar "Manni." Standing: Mate to "Nikili," (seen in "Costumed Animals"). 10"/25 cm., mohair; jointed head and arms; white felt body; felt shorts (snap closure) and yellow shoes; yellow print bowtie; missing vest, ca. 1958. Rare in mint condition. Courtesy Nancy Crane.

170

"Pummy"; 10″/25 cm. (incl. ears), No. 2960/25, straw stuffed, jointed head only, long pile white mohair airbrushed in shades of grey; brown glass eyes. Mint, ca. 1960s. Desirable. "Pummy" and "Ossi" are the same design; the latter is in shades of brown. Courtesy Dee Hockenberry.

"Vario" Rabbit: 6½″/17 cm., No. 3070/17, cream color mohair, straw stuffed, jointed head and back legs making him exceedingly posable; brown glass eyes, black floss nose/mouth, ca. 1960 (can have either raised or incised button). Courtesy Dee Hockenberry.

Black lambs: Right, "Lamby," 5½″/14 cm. and 8½″/22 cm., wool plush with light yellow/green glass eyes, white tail and face; bell. Left, "Swapl" the Persian black Lamb; 4″/10 cm. is all wool plush; the 5½″/14 cm. size has a mohair face and wool plush body. The two largest sizes, 10″/25 cm. and 13″/33 cm. are all mohair with a curly "Persian" wool look. Not shown is the 8½″/22 cm. that is similar to the 5½″/14 cm. size. All of the "Swapl" black lambs have *blue* eyes and black tails and *no* bell. "Swapl" is more common than the black "Lamby." Both are hard to find in the larger sizes, ca. late 1950s. Courtesy Jane L. Viprino.

Wild Animals

Uncatalogued treasures; the most coveted of the Steiff pet animals because of extreme rarity. "Brosus," (Brontosaurus): 12"/30.5 cm. long, No. 1315,90, yellow mohair belly ruled with brown, grey mohair back gloriously airbrushed with brown, blues, orange and yellows. The existing fossil dinosaur skins do not show color patterns; Steiff took artistic license. Lime green and black glass googly eyes were used. The open mouth is pink felt/painted teeth above. The spine (orange felt) is not anatomically correct. Brontosaurus was the largest land animal that ever lived; 60-80 ft. long with a body weight of 30-50 tons. He was a vegetarian and roamed the earth 150 million years ago. Today he is the logo for the Sinclair Oil Co. "Dinos," (Stegosauras): 12"/30.5 cm. long, No. 1312,90, also known as the "plated dinosaur," had *two* rows of triangular-shaped bony plates down the center back (Steiff used *one* row of painted felt); yellow mohair belly ruled with brown, the entire back is a kaleidoscope of color in shades of blue, emerald green, brown, magenta and yellow; green and black glass googly eyes, pink felt open mouth/painted teeth; yellow felt flanges. "Dinos" neck is far too long for this creature and Steiff omitted the 4 spikes on tail (used for defense). This reptile was 20

ft. long, a vegetarian and lived 130-180 million years ago. "Tysus," (Tyrannosaurus): 8"/20 cm. high, No. 4317,90, yellow, orange, turquoise, brown and beige markings on mohair; black and white glass googly eyes; light orange felt open mouth/painted teeth. The movable arms are the only jointing among the three animals. The green felt spine is anatomically incorrect. Tyrannosaurus Rex was the king of the dinosaurs and the largest land-living meat-eater of all time. He stood 20 ft. high and was 40 ft. long with a body weight of 6-8 tons. This carnivore lived 135-170 million years ago. The larger of the two sizes (17"/43 cm. - 29"/73.5 cm.) are seen in the 1958 F.A.O. Schwarz catalogue. The 12"/30.5 cm. size did not appear. There is no indication they were an F.A.O. Schwarz "exclusive." A 12 ft. long (store display) size has also been seen. This model could be dismantled for transport. In the late '50s, the small size retailed for $6.00; the larger for $15.00-18.00. "Dinos" is the most common; the most lavish, the best seller and more were made. "Tysus" has the most demand; jointed arms and he was king. "Brosus" is the most rare. All in store new condition with raised script buttons and C.T. (Author).

Velvet squirrels, the precursor of "Possy," (see Vol. I, pg. 274): 4"/10 cm., No. 4410; left, brown velvet with plastic eyes; right, grey velvet with glass eyes; both have bushy mohair tails and ears, delicate airbrushed markings and are straw stuffed. Made only 1950s to 1956, they are rare. Note difference in value is due to differences in condition. Courtesy Kirk Stines.

Skunk: 4″/10 cm. long, No. 1410,00 (one size only); black and white mohair/black velvet underside, straw stuffed, unjointed; brown glass eyes, pink twisted floss nose/mouth. Rare and desirable, ca. 1958-1963. Courtesy Dee Hockenberry.

Bumble Bee: 16″/40.5 cm., yellow and black cotton plush, stuffed with grey reprocessed cotton; unjointed; vinyl mask face with Kewpie smile, yellow felt wings/black designs; black felt wired antennae. Possible Gund, ca. 1950. (Author).

"Mockie," 4″/10 cm., No. 1310 (note the repeat of numbers); grey mohair; straw stuffed; glass googly eyes; open felt mouth; yarn tail, ca. early 1950s-early 1960s. Because of its inherent humorous appearance, the hippo is a popular animal. Courtesy Carolyn Altfather.

So-called "Bengal Tiger," 5½"/14 cm. high, No. 3314; tigered mohair; straw stuffed, unjointed; green glass eyes, rose color twisted floss nose, open felt mouth with painted outline; nylon whiskers. Also made with teeth in 8½"/22 cm. and 17"/43 cm. sizes, but the miniature is the most desirable. Note the detailed contouring and brushwork. Rare, ca. 1959. (Author).

Bengal Tiger cub: 4"/10 cm. high, No. 5310, yellow tigered mohair, straw stuffed, f.j., green glass eyes; pink painted nose and mouth outlined in black floss; *brown* floss claws, stiff nylon filament whiskers; raised script button, ca. 1950s. Full jointing is desirable. (Author).

Papa lion of the fully jointed Lion Family; 8½"/22 cm. long; yellow and brown mohair, straw stuffed, glass eyes, rose twisted floss nose, black mouth; ca. late 1950s. (See Cub, Vol. I, pg. 266). Of the many Steiff "Large Cats", these small, fully jointed examples are in greatest demand. Courtesy Dee Hockenberry.

"Luxy" Desert Lynx (also called Persian Lynx): 10″/25 cm. high, No. 3325,00; sitting posture; note the broad feet; tan/white moahir with black ear tufts; orange glass eyes for hunting at night. Also made in 6½″/17 cm. size. Rare, ca. 1963. Zebra: Old cotton plush, printed Steiff button "ff" underscored, ca. 1940. Note the older Steiff animals have a thinner, more realistic conformation. Courtesy Jane L. Viprino.

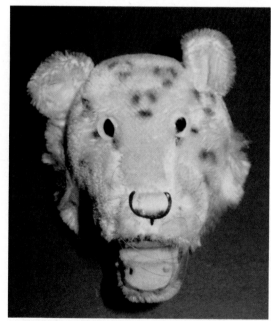

Reclining leopard, 5½″/10 cm. high, No. 1310,00, golden mohair marked with 4 or 5 dark brown spots in rosettes, straw stuffed, green plastic "glow-in-the-dark" eyes, rose twisted floss nose, black floss claws. Made from late 1950s to early 1960s; probably discontinued to make way for its look-alike cousin, the ocelot, which was introduced in 1964. Leopard standing, 5½″ long, No. 1314; mohair, straw stuffed, green glass eyes, rose floss nose. Among the miniatures of "Large Cats" in standing posture, the lioness is the most rare. Courtesy Kirk Stines.

"Look-alike" Steiff Trophy Head, made in Japan: 6″/15 cm. high head, 3¼″/8 cm. oval, soft wood backing stained pink. Steiff used a slightly larger unstained *hardwood* oval, 4″/10 cm. (see Elephant Trophy Head, Vol I, pg. 259). Both have straw stuffing and mohair; the leopard spots (in groups of 3) are *sparse* but correct; the whiskers are *limp* nylon thread instead of fishing line weight; *thin* felt lines the open mouth with missing teeth; ears are *sliced* into head (a time saving device); but the primary clue is that the nose is stitched with tell-tale pink single ply *thread*. Focus on the nose stitching when identifying an animal. These Japanese Trophy Heads appear as other jungle animals also. Courtesy Nancy Roeder.

"Loopy," wolf: 13½"/34 cm. high, raised script button; grey/brown mohair; open mouth with red felt tongue, plastic teeth. A 10"/25 cm. size was also made. Extremely rare and valued accordingly. The conformation is similar to the standing open mouth Police Dog "Arco", ca. late 1950s. "Original Steiff" mohair panda: 4½"/11 cm., flexible limbs, incised ear button, ca. late 1960s. Courtesy Jane L. Viprino.

"Diggy," badger on all fours: 6"/15 cm. long and 12"/30.5 cm.; white/brown/black mohair, the luxuriant pelt of the badger is brought to life in these striking examples, ca. early 1960s. Once again, the small is common; the large is rare. Courtesy Jane L. Viprino.

Texas Longhorn Steer: 9"/23 cm. high, 13"/33 cm. long; tan/brown mohair; googly glass eyes; *leather* over wire horns. Rare, ca. 1962. "Yuku" gazelle: 8½"/22 cm. high, No. 1322,00; golden and white mohair with vinyl horns; black shoe button-like eyes. This well rendered fleet-footed small antelope also came in 12"/30.5 cm. size. Rare. Courtesy Jane L. Viprino.

Humanized Steiff tiger: 36″/91 cm., tigered mohair, straw and cotton stuffed, f.j., green glass eyes, "Steiff rose color" twisted floss nose, nylon whiskers; airbrushed markings on mohair pads; mitten type mohair hands. This oversized Lulac-type, ca. late 1950s, is irresistible as well as very rare. Courtesy Ellyn McCorkell.

"Sulac," Cocker Spaniel: 15½″/40 cm., No. 7340, mohair in shades of gold, staw and cotton stuffed, f.j., dangling legs. "Zolac," Zotty Bear: 15½″/40 cm., also No. 7340 (same as above). A black tom cat "Kolac" was made as well, ca. 1964, when Steiff's exports were down. Therefore, these and many rare and hard-to-find animals date from that year. "Lulac" 15½″/40 cm., mohair, came later and was made for a longer period of time. Note all have chest plates. By 1974 there was a large "Lulac" made of mink imitation plush. Courtesy Robin Lowe.

"Wiggy" (white) and "Waggy" (brown) can be seen in their winter and summer coats. These flat-footed members of the weasel family are rare and unique: 7″/17.5 cm. long, No. 1612,04 and No. 1612,03. Raised script ear button; Dralon with pipe cleaner tails which are often missing. Courtesy Jane L. Viprino.

Red Fox: 11″/28 cm. high, 17″/43 cm. long, No. 1328,00; mohair; straw stuffed; glass eyes. Steiff is noted for their beautiful foxes. Rarely seen large size, ca. 1959-1960. Courtesy Robin Lowe.

"Nelly," snail, falls into the "exotic" category: 4"/10 cm. high, No. 2410; made in either pinkish brown or bluish green spotted velvet; leatherette underside; colorful vinyl shell; flexible vinyl antennae with knob on end. These protrusions are easily broken. One black glass bead eye is replaced. Production can be pinpointed to 1961-1963 *only*. *Very* rare and fascinating member of the Steiff menagerie. (Author).

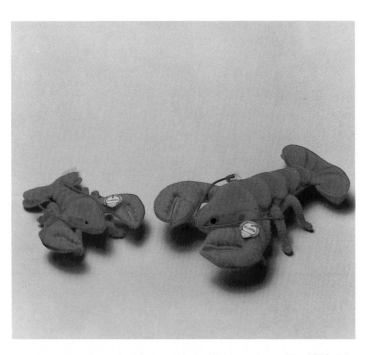

"Crabby," lobster: 1½"/3.5 cm. high, 4"/10 cm. long, No. 2010; felt with pipe cleaner legs, straw stuffed, plastic eyes, exquisite airbrushed markings; came mint-in-bag with raised script button. Larger: 2½"/6.3 cm. high, 7"/17 cm. long; same as above. Rare, ca. 1963-1965. However, the *all mohair* lobster (see Vol. I, pg. 258) is even more rare. Courtesy Kirk Stines.

Steiff as a keen observer of nature, sitting frogs: Large, 11"/28 cm. high, No. 3328 (also made in 8"/20 cm. size); small, 3¼"/08 cm. and 4"/10 cm. The large is green mohair, the small are green velvet; airbrushed dark brown markings; gold mohair or velvet undersides; straw stuffed; unjointed; *gold* glass stick pin eyes. Because of the elaborate contouring and decoration, sitting frogs are in demand—yet can be found. The smallest example has the old printed button "ff" underscored. Steiff has made frogs since 1934 and all seem different. A plausible explanation: A stencil would wear out at the factory and another would be cut on the spot. Therefore, we see variations in the brush design. (Author).

Lesser Panda, "Pandy," listed as "Indian Panda" in the 1963-1964 catalog: 4"/20 cm. high, No. 1310,00, and 8"/20 cm. high; a 6"/15 cm. size was also made. Orange and black mohair, straw stuffed, swivel head, glass eyes, floss nose; raised script ear buttons. In 1964 the 4"/10 cm. size retailed for $3.75; extremely rare and coveted now. Lesser Pandas, members of the racoon family, live in forests in the Himalaya Mountains. Courtesy Jane L. Viprino.

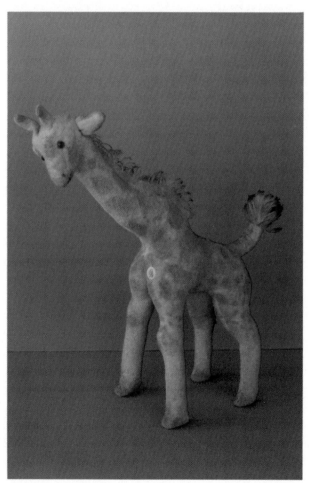

"Xorry" or "Desert Fox," 6½"/17 cm. sitting, No. 3317 (also made in "miniature size" 5"/12 cm.); orange and white mohair, straw stuffed, unjointed; glass eyes and black twisted floss nose, ca. 1960s. Note the sweet face of a kit with "alert" ears. Courtesy Dee Hockenberry.

"Petz" giraffe with milk glass chest button: 10"/25 cm., spotted *cotton* coat; long mohair mane and tail; felt ears and horns; glass eyes. Artistic example, ca. late 1950s. There is little known about the Petz soft toys. Collectors have only recently realized there was a German company by that name. Courtesy Nan C. Moorehead.

Petz monkey: 8½″/22 cm., long white mohair frosted brown; f.j.; tan felt face, ears and paws; glass eyes. Note the milk glass "Petz" button on wire stem in chest; tagged on arm, "6/8." Made in Germany, ca. 1950s. Courtesy Nan C. Moorehead.

Green monkey with pixie face: 4″/10 cm. high, 4″/10 cm. long, white mohair airbrushed gloriously in shades of green, blue, orange and gold (the markings are similar to Steiff's "Mungo" but *not exactly);* swivel head, *clear* glass eyes appearing blue due to the intense color of painted upper face. The white *felt* ears are shaded pink and the *felt* feet have stitched toes with separate thumb. Variations related to sizes of Steiff toys can lead to legitimate differences in features. However, this miniature is an uncatalogued size for Steiff. Maker unknown. (Author).

"Mungo," 10″/25 cm., No. 1325,07, white mohair airbrushed in shades of green, orange and blue; straw stuffed, jointed head, wire armature in arms and tail; squeaker. The distinguishing feature is the blue glass eyes. "Mungo's" colors tend to fade. Common, ca. late 1950s-1960s. Retailed for $8.25 in 1964; the middle of 3 sizes. Steiff's production quantities for all animals: The ratio of medium or small sizes to the largest size is 2 or 3 to 1. Courtesy Claudia Shotwell.

Dangling Orangutan: 12″/30 cm., No. 0060/30, reddish brown Crylor, loosely stuffed with wool and foam rubber making him easy to pose; vinyl molded and painted face, knitted jersey-type covered feet and hands that are sewn closed, ca. 1971. Steiff has captured the essence of the orangutan: they avoid walking and with an arm spread of 8 ft., they swing gracefully through the trees. **Hard to find but little demand.** Courtesy Nancy Roeder.

Of the many Steiff post-WW II elephants, this large TV animal is one of the most rare. "Snuggy Jumbo," 22″/55 cm., No. 7355, grey mohair with airbrushed markings; steel frame; black/white glass eyes; open mouth, felt tusks; tan suede-like pads; red felt saddle; raised script button, ca. 1957. Courtesy Dee Hockenberry.

"Dormy," Dormouse, an old world rodent resembling a squirrel: 8″/20 cm. long, No. 2220/20, (also made in 5″/12 cm. size); long pile mohair (68% wool, 32% cotton) tipped in browns; light pink synthetic plush inset face; soft stuffed body in curled position; black shiny plastic eyes; floss and painted nose/mouth; nylon whiskers. Note the unusual placement of chest tag, ca. 1960-1970. Rodent-types are not the most popular collectible. In 1985 "Dormy" is a rabbit. (Author).

"Cosy Raggy," 8″/20 cm., No. 4820/20, incised button; Dralon stuffed with foam (as all Cosys are); jointed head, plastic eyes, floss nose. This 1972 to 1978 racoon replaced "Cosy Raccy" made 1957-1971. "Cosy" means "petable" from the German *kosen*. An attractive toy aimed at the Steiff consumer in Germany - the children. Courtesy Kirk Stines.

Gebr. Hermann prairie dog: 6″/15 cm. high; long pile blonde mohair, sheared mohair head with airbrushed markings; soft stuffed, unjointed; amber plastic eyes; stitched nose/mouth; peach felt ears and cut-out feet. Note the life-like appearance. Chest tag, ca. 1960-1970. Courtesy Ellyn McCorkell.

Gebr. Hermann fawn: 10″/25 cm. high, 6″/15 cm. long; short pile mohair, straw stuffed, unjointed, black glass eyes; gold tag, ca. 1960s. Note the *embroidery style* of the nose often seen on Gebr. Hermann animals. Courtesy Kay Bransky.

"Trampy," a new item in 1975: 6½″/17 cm., No. 0510/17 (also made in 11″/28 cm. size); Trevira velvet stuffed with polyurethane foam, brown plastic eyes, plastic tusks, felt ears, airbrushed toes. The oversized head and trunk give the illusion of a comical young elephant. The hole in the ear was left by removal of the riveted button, not by a pygmy arrow. Courtesy Carolyn Altfather.

A splendid collection of various sizes and materials of Gemse (also called Alpine Goat) and Rocky Steinbock (also called Mountain Ram or Ibex). The large curving horns of Rocky are unmistakable. In either mohair or Trevira velvet, the Gemse with the small dark horns is also recognizable. Note that the mother and baby Gemse have tails of *bristle* rather than the fabric tails of the other animals. This baby is easy to identify among the range of Steiff goats and sheep because of the unique tail. Left front (clockwise): "Alpine Goat," 5″/12 cm., mohair, bristle tail, ca. 1969. Mother "Alpine Goat," 6½″/17 cm., mohair, bristle tail, ca. 1969. "Mountain Ram," 8½″/22 cm., mohair with line ruled felt horns, ca. 1969. "Alpine Goat," also called "Chamois," 8½″/22 cm., Trevira velvet, ca. 1978. "Mountain Ram," 5½″/14 cm., mohair, line ruled felt horns, ca. 1969. "Mountain Ram," 8½″/22 cm., Trevira velvet, ca. 1978. "Alpine Goat," 5½″/14 cm., Trevira velvet, ca. 1978. "Mountain Ram," also called "Rocky Mountain Sheep," 5½″/15 cm., Trevira velvet, ca. 1978. The *Trevira-samt* (knitted velvet) animals have an appeal to some. The airbrushing is more exact, and the short nap on the woven fabric is to the scale of small animals. All courtesy Carolyn Altfather.

Life-size giraffe: 94½″/240 cm., No. 0759/24, note the open mouth on this, ca. 1981, STUDIO animal. In 1986 the mouth was closed. There is one man at the Steiff factory who has the difficult task of bending the heavy metal frames. There is also a baby giraffe, 59″/150 cm. These are often purchased, for example, by young couples furnishing a sun room; made to order. Courtesy Beth Savino, Hobby Center Toys.

Steiff Birds

Penguin: 4″/10 cm., No. 4310, (also made in 5½″/14 cm. and 8½″/22 cm. sizes); black and white mohair with *velvet* wings; straw stuffed; unjointed; glass eyes; felt feet and beak, ca. early 1950s to 1956. This rare penguin with the white stripe on head was replaced by the more familiar "Peggy" in 1957; posed in front of *Animal Toys*, published by Brimax Books, England. Courtesy Kirk Stines.

"Peggy," 8½″/22 cm., No. 2500/22; mohair body (59% wool, 41% cotton) in shades of blue, green, yellow and black. These colors are set off by a red felt beak and small brown eyes; swivel head; suede-type feet. Made in 4 sizes, "Peggy" was a good seller because of her beauty, so enjoyed a long production life, ca. 1960 on. Very common. (Author).

"Adebar," stork, 6½″/17 cm., No. 1117, white felt covered body, black felt tail, straw stuffed, glass eyes, plastic beak; wire legs and feet; a great favorite among collectors; also made in 13½″/35 cm. and 24″/60 cm. sizes. Mint, ca. late 1950s; phased out 1970/1971. Courtesy Dee Hockenberry.

"Piccy" pelican: 6½″/17 cm., No. 1317,00; beautiful light pink coloring to the mohair (often found to be faded); straw stuffed body; the flapable wings are soft stuffed; glass googly eyes, felt feet and beak which is edged with vinyl; raised script button; made 1959 to early 1960s. Rare and desirable. Courtesy Kirk Stines.

Hen, standing 4″/10 cm., No. 1310, gold mohair/black markings, straw stuffed, felt comb, face and wattle; metal legs and feet. Also made in 6½″/17 cm. size with felt feet. Raised script Steiff button, old C.T. Courtesy Dee Hockenberry.

Cosy spotted chicken: 5″/12 cm. No. 3385/12; cosy plush (80% Dralon, 20% cotton) is easily matted. "Cosy" soft toys are worth one half as much as mohair; made as baby's playthings, there is little demand. However, this chick with *plastic* feet has his own special personality, ca. 1970. An all-yellow cosy chick was also made. Courtesy Rosemary Moran.

"Floppy Hen," 6″/15 cm., No. 7328, white mohair decorated in shades of peach and gold, unjointed, softly stuffed; felt face and trim; brown floss sleeping eyes (characteristic of the "Floppy" series). In nesting position, the wings have parallel machine stitching on tips to accent feathers. Raised script Steiff button underside left wing. The hen had a short life (1958-1961) and was featured on the cover of the 1958 Easter catalogue. "Rooster," 11½″/28 cm., No. 3350/28, body is mohair dramatically painted in shades of orange, gold and black; red felt wattle and comb; black button eyes; peach felt legs and feet over a wire armature. Steiff button is attached to the green felt tail plume, This is the largest of 3 sizes. Visual bird, ca. 1968. (Author).

Ravens: 3½″/9 cm. wool Pom-Pom described on page 186. "Hucky" 5″/12 cm., No. 7312, raised script button; black mohair body and felt wings/tail feathers, straw stuffed, jointed head, plastic eyes, orange felt beak, wire legs/feet; made from mid-1950s to 1976 (the last 2 years with plastic feet). When the Steiff factory repaired the metal feet they replaced his old chest tag with the present day red/yellow tag. Easy to find. Courtesy Kirk Stines.

Waterfowl as popular collector items: Left, 4″/10 cm. No. 3250/10, incised button, made 1965-1976; yellow mohair, straw stuffed, plastic eyes, felt bill and feet. Goose, 6½″/17 cm., No. 6317, rasied script button, US-Zone tag (made 1945-1952); standing, mohair, straw stuffed, glass eyes, felt beak, tail and feet; no sign of chest tag yet mint condition. Note, yellow I.D. tags on US-Zone pieces say, "Original *geschutzt*", (protected by law or copyright). Colored duck: 8″/18 cm., No. 6317, raised script button, US-Zone tag; standing, brightly colored mohair, straw stuffed, glass eyes, felt feet and bill, non-working squeaker; rare to find US-Zone pieces in this mint condition; no sign of a chest tag. Courtesy Kirk Stines.

"Finch," 5″/12 cm., No. 1312,3; mohair in colors; glass eyes; plastic beak; metal feet; double weight felt wings and tail; also made in 6½″/17 cm. size, ca. 1960. Raised script button. Hard to find. Courtesy Chris McWilliams.

Wool "Pom-Pom" birds and animals: Top row, Colored duck, 2½″/6.4 cm., No. 1506b, wool, glass eyes, felt bill, metal feet; early 1950s to late 1960s; pair of birds, 1½″/3.8 cm., No. 6504, 2, wool, glass eyes, felt beak and tail, early 1950s, metal feet replaced by plastic in 1957; Raven, 3½″/9 cm., No. 1508, wool, glass googly eyes, felt beak and tail, metal feet (replaced by plastic in early 1970s); made early 1950s to late 1960s; yellow duck, 2½″/6.4 cm. No. 150G, wool, glass eyes, felt bill, metal feet, raised script button, ca. early 1950s to late 1960s; white rabbit, 2½″/6.4 cm., No. 2504,1, raised script button, wool, glass eyes, felt ears, made early 1950s to 1965. Bottom row: grey and white rabbit, 2½″/6.4 cm., No. 2504, 1, raised script button, wool, glass eyes, felt ears, made early 1950s to 1965. Bottom row: grey and white rabbit, 2½″/6.4 cm., No. 2504, 5, wool, glass eyes, felt ears, ca. early 1950s to 1965; "Ladybug," 2″/5 cm., No. 1504, wool, glass eyes, ca. early 1950s to 1965; Seagull, 3″/7.5 cm., No. 1508, wool, glass eyes, felt beak and tail, metal feet, raised script button, ca. 1957. Pom-Pom toys have seen little change since the 1930s. Courtesy Kirk Stines.

White pigeon, 10″/25 cm. high, 8″/20 cm. long, No. 2564/25 (also made in grey); white Dralon, white felt fan-tail with pale blue shadow detailing, felt lower half of wing; pink circle of felt backs black plastic eyes; pink plastic beak and feet. Button incised, ca. 1969. Courtesy Carolyn Altfather.

"Screech Owl," 11½″/28 cm., No. 2593/28, STUDIO: Covering is 90% acrylic, 10% cotton; unjointed; large gold plastic eyes, soft plastic beak; double weight grey felt soles on large feet. Decorations are stenciled onto the bolt of fabric and highlighted after construction. New issue in 1982. The incised brass button has begun to tarnish. Retail price, 1985, $99.00. Courtesy Mary Alice Carey.

Made as favors for a child's Easter basket (aesthetically appreciated now): Stork, 4¼″/11 cm., No. 7460/11, 100% wool, plastic beak and feet, ca. 1975. Wool goose: 2″/05 cm., No. 2505,44, 100% wool, felt beak, wings and feet, ca. 1968. All courtesy Carolyn Altfather.

"Lora" parrot, 8½"/22 cm. high, No. 2520/22; red mohair body and tail, inset of blue mohair under tail and on wings that are airbrushed with turquoise and gold; honey-combed chest; green plastic eyes rimmed in black; white felt face plate, soft vinyl beak; striped tan felt feet. Also made in 5"/12 cm. size; a long production period ending 1974-1975. Hard to find mint. The clown-like behavior and mimicking voice have endeared them as pets and now as a decorative toy. Hand-stitched rag doll, 19"/48 cm., sawdust stuffed, brown calico dress, quilted petticoat, red stroud cloth stockings, ca. 1850. (Author).

"Stanli," drake, 12"/30 cm. high, 15"/38 cm. long, Dralon, black plastic eyes, felt bill; another example of the beautifully detailed Steiff birds made for a short time, ca. 1973. Courtesy Dee Hockenberry.

Swan, 10½"/26 cm., No. 3247/26, smaller incised brass button (0.8 cm.) with paper tag, white synthetic plush (70% acrylic, 30% cotton), brown plastic eyes, orange velvet beak, black velvet face and feet; white felt wing tips. A white all-felt swan was made in the early years but acrylic lends itself better to feathers. Striking bird, ca. 1980s; discontinued 1986. In 1985 a 8"/20 cm. white swan with *orange* feet appeared together with a 8"/20 cm. *black* swan that lasted only 1 year. Rare already. (Author).

Red Chinese Pheasant: 16″/40 cm. high, 30″/76 cm. long; STUDIO display animal listed as "Golden Pheasant" in 1979-1983. Made of Dralon. Steiff has discontinued some of their STUDIO line; however, models solely for home decor will continue to be available. Courtesy Jane L. Viprino.

"Tucky," turkey: 4″/10 cm. (a 6″/15 cm. size also made). Colorful mohair and felt with metal legs. Hard to find, ca. 1960s. Cosy Ente (Duck Boy) dressed as a sailor: 10″/25 cm. No. 4907/25, Dralon. A girl sailor duck was also made, ca. 1970. Courtesy Jane L. Viprino.

Green woodpecker: 11″/28 cm., No. 2604/28, STUDIO: Body is 60% acrylic, 40% cotton in shades of green; stiffened and stamped brown felt wings and tail; black and white face with red top knot; yellow plastic eyes; hard plastic beak, White felt feet have long extending wires that were factory-attached through the tree limb to secure bird to this prop. An even more beautiful spotted woodpecker was made at the same time (1980-1982). A good example of: "Rare does not have to be old." Distribution was focused to Europe. (Author).

"Putty" Turkey, 5½″/14 cm., No. 3367/14: A staggering list of textures and colors (brown, green, red, gold, black and white). Body is 75% acrylic, 25% cotton plush in black and white with sides of brown; emerald green plush at rear tail center and lower breast; flesh-colored jersey knit head and neck, single weight red felt wattle and comb; chocolate brown felt tail and wings stamped with a feather design; thick white felt beak; small brown plastic eyes; plastic feet. Mainly European distribution, ca. 1980-1983. Rare and beautiful. Courtesy Mary Alice Carey.

"Franzi," parakeet: 5¼″/13 cm., No. 2534/13; electric blue Trevira velvet with airbrushed markings; felt brush tail; plastic eyes, beak and feet. Her mate named "Hansi" was green and yellow. This design was made from 1950s-1974/1975 of velveteen; 1975 - present of Trevira (synthetic) velvet; none the less beautiful for a long life. Courtesy Carolyn Altfather.

Price Guides

Revised Price Guide for Teddy Bears & Steiff Animals

Page 20 & 21
Acrobatic Bear........400.00
Ferriswheel Pair.......600.00
Tin Plate...............95.00
Teddy Bear button......15.00
6″ Japanese............35.00
3½″ Steiff, 1910......400.00
8″ Mohair............350.00

Page 22 & 23
3¾″ Mohair..........450.00
5″ Hermann..........250.00
5″ Imported.........150.00
Bathing Bear..........75.00
5½″ Bear on Wheels...25.00
4″ Honey Mohair.....150.00

Page 24 & 25
Beige Mohair........400.00
Clown...............25.00
Yellowstone Bear.....85.00
Pink Bear...........45.00

Page 26 & 27
Postcards........10.00-15.00
5½″ German Wind-up...45.00
Christmas Ornament.....6.00
2½″ Teddy...........25.00
Teddy Bear School.....65.00
Japanese Mini Bears.ea. 35.00
6½″ Steiff..........275.00
5½″ Steiff..........200.00
6″ Steiff...........200.00

Page 28 & 29
Walking Bear.........35.00
6″ Bear.............15.00
Snow White Steiff.....350.00
3½″ Steiff, left.....300.00
3½″ Steiff, right....250.00
Jackie......600.00-700.00

Page 30 & 31
Hermann Bears.....ea. 125.00
6″ Dark Mohair......200.00
Young Bear..........125.00
The Graduate.........55.00
Drummer.............55.00
7″ Petz Bear.......115.00
Wooden Swing........20.00
Teddy Bear Bottle....20.00

Page 32 & 33
3½″ Steiff Teddy.....200.00
White Mohair........225.00
Beige Mohair........200.00
6″ Teddy Bears..175.00-200.00
Brown Bear..........20.00

Page 34 & 35
Oil Cloth Bear........20.00
Tabby...............35.00
Mohair Bear..........55.00
Snap Bear.............2.00

Page 36
Bisque Doll.........150.00
Total of Bears......575.00

Page 38 & 39
28″ White Mohair.....2,000.00
White Mohair.3,500.00-4,500.00

Page 40 & 41
16″ Blonde Mohair...1,600.00
13″ Steiff..........1,600.00
Teddy Bears Book.....250.00
16″ Gold Mohair.....2,000.00

Page 42 & 43
Emerson...........2,500.00
20″ Steiff.........2,100.00
Dark Brown Steiff...1,300.00
Little Brown Bear Book...65.00

Page 44 & 45
1905 Mohair.....1,100.00
12″ Mohair.........650.00
Cloth Bear.........195.00
13″ Mohair.........700.00

Page 46 & 47
1907 12″ Steiff.......900.00
12″ Gold Mohair......650.00
21″ Mohair..........600.00
13″ Steiff........1,600.00

Page 48 & 49
Beguiling Bear......600.00
13″ Steiff........1,300.00
3½″ Steiff.........300.00
Blanket.............35.00
14″ Steiff........1,400.00
Petsy..............150.00
15″ Mohair.........800.00

Page 50 & 51
12″ Steiff.........475.00
14″ Mohair.......1,100.00
12″ Mohair.........700.00

Page 52 & 53
16″ Brown Bear.....800.00
12″ Steiff.........800.00
11″ Teddy..........600.00

Page 54 & 55
19″ Steiff.......1,400.00
14″ Mohair.........700.00

Page 56 & 57
Lucky..............600.00
14″ Steiff........1,500.00

Page 58 & 59
Twins..........pr. 900.00
Roosevelt Bear......900.00
15″ Mohair.........100.00
14″ Mohair.........350.00

Page 60 & 61
10″ Steiff.........900.00
10″ Mohair.........900.00
Louie............1,300.00
15″ Mohair.........800.00

Page 62 & 63
Steiff Bear........700.00
English Bear.......700.00
12″ Steiff.........900.00

Page 64 & 65
9½″ Mohair.........400.00
8″ Mohair..........300.00
12″ Mohair.........600.00
Cow, horse & pig....ea. 35.00
Rooster............55.00
Madonna............800.00
Child..............350.00

Page 66 & 67
21″ Mohair.......1,400.00
22″ Mohair.......1,200.00
12″ Mohair.........900.00
Doll...............50.00
16″ Mohair.........800.00
Viewer and Cards....125.00

Page 68 & 69
Grover Cleveland.....800.00
13″ Mohair.........900.00

Page 70 & 71
12″ Steiff.......1,000.00
12″ White Mohair....650.00
Minerva............350.00
Bear Boy...........150.00
Fur Bear Boy.......135.00
Tin Horse Cart......45.00

Page 72 & 73
12″ Horsman........400.00
13″ Mohair.........700.00
Protective Bear....550.00
18″ Mohair.........900.00

Page 74 & 75
Early Bear.........900.00
10″ Mohair.........250.00
12″ White Mohair....250.00
10″ Irresistible Bear...650.00

Page 76 & 77
Smug Bear..........350.00

Page 78 & 79
10″ Steiff.........750.00
16″ Mohair.........800.00
15″ Mohair.........750.00

Page 78 & 79
21″ Mohair......1,000.00
1915 Steiff, top....1,200.00
1915 Steiff, bottom....1,200.00

Page 80 & 81
12″ Mohair.........350.00
17″ Mohair.........850.00
21″ Electric Eye Bear...650.00

Page 82 & 83
22″ Electric Eye Bear...625.00
Novelty Bear........750.00
Patriotic Bear......600.00
Black Bear..........800.00

Page 84 & 85
Steiff Clown Bear....900.00
24″ Mohair.........800.00
Book...............185.00
Super Teddy........750.00
Book...............95.00
Fillmore...........700.00

Page 86 & 87
12″ Mohair.........450.00
13″ Mohair.........650.00
11″ Mohair.........600.00
24″ Beige Bear....1,650.00
Mama Bear..........650.00
Papa Bear........1,800.00
Baby Bear..........175.00

Page 88 & 89
14″ Mohair.........700.00
14″ Steiff.......1,050.00
9″ Mohair..........150.00
Poker Face.........600.00

Page 90 & 91
Mrs. Roosevelt......950.00
20″ Steiff.........500.00
23″ Sailor cloth....400.00

Page 92 & 93
17″ Mohair.........500.00
23″ American.....1,000.00
10″ White Mohair....300.00
18″ Mohair.......1,000.00

Page 94 & 95
Shy Bear...........600.00
Horse..............150.00
Doll's Bear........550.00
Early American Teddy...425.00
Elephant...........600.00
Snowball...........700.00

Page 96 & 97
18″ Mohair.........900.00
Teacher............600.00
Book...............95.00
21″ Mohair.........600.00
6″ Mohair..........200.00

Page 98 & 99
18″ Mohair.........650.00
14½″ Bear.........600.00
15½″ Bear.........700.00
26″ Mohair.......2,000.00
22″ Mohair.........650.00

Page 100 & 101
Mechanical Bears...ea. 550.00
Dr. O'Bear.........550.00
15″ Mohair.........450.00
9½″ Steiff.........700.00

Page 102 & 103
Steiff Clown Bear....600.00
13″ Mohair.........400.00
Dog................75.00
Bellhop Bear.......275.00

Page 104 & 105
13″ Mohair.........700.00
12″ Mohair.........700.00
13″ Bear...........175.00

Page 106 & 107
16″ Mohair.........400.00
14″ Angora Mohair...350.00

Page 106 & 107
24″ White Mohair....700.00
20″ Mohair.........900.00
Sitting dog........125.00
Polish Bear.........25.00
Mr. Wheatly........750.00

Page 108 & 109
Old Fellow.........350.00
13″ Mohair.........325.00
Bearskin...........20.00
Block..............10.00
12″ Brown Bear.....350.00
Horse..............75.00
Donkey.............125.00
"See-Saw"...........35.00
Gold Bear..........525.00

Page 110 & 111
13″ Brown Bear.....425.00
23″ Mohair.........375.00
30″ Circus Bear....350.00
22″ Circus Bear.....75.00

Page 112 & 113
18″ Mohair.........375.00
16″ White Mohair....450.00
16″ Gold Mohair....325.00
Trunk..............40.00
Mama Bear..........175.00
Baby Bear..........125.00
16″ Golden Mohair...800.00
17″ Red Mohair.....475.00

Page 114 & 115
Ted................275.00
15″ Red, White & Blue..500.00
24″ Gold Mohair....675.00
Helvetic Bear....1,000.00
18″ Mohair.........400.00

Page 116 & 117
Pink Mohair........300.00
Red Mohair.........200.00
Book...............95.00
Brown Mohair.......325.00
English Bear.......500.00
Book...............150.00

Page 118 & 119
21″ Mohair.........550.00
9″ Silver-grey Mohair...675.00
19″ Carmel Mohair...550.00
24″ Mohair.........600.00
Red Coat Bear......550.00
22″ Gold Mohair....500.00

Page 120 & 121
20″ Gold Mohair....600.00
18″ Grey Mohair....550.00
17″ White Mohair...425.00
16″ Telephone Teddy...325.00
17″ Telephone Teddy...500.00
15″ Thin Bear......450.00

Page 122 & 123
Steam Roller Bear.....450.00
Steam Roller.......150.00
10″ White Mohair...150.00
13″ Standing Bear...175.00
12″ Seated Bear....175.00
Tuxedo Bear........200.00

Page 124 & 125
Magician...........350.00
19″ Gold Mohair....375.00
19″ Cinnamon Mohair...375.00
16″ Gold Mohair....300.00
English Twins......pr. 600.00

Page 126 & 127
12″ Gold Mohair....150.00
13″ Gold Mohair.....85.00
Drum Major..........45.00
Twins.............pr. 550.00
23″ Seated Bear....550.00

21" Standing Bear....325.00
12" Younger Bear......125.00
15" Steiff...........600.00
Page 128 & 129
Baby Faced Bear........25.00
13" Bear.............175.00
Old Timer............300.00
My Teddy.............450.00
Page 130 & 131
20" White Mohair.....500.00
14" Yellow Mohair....350.00
Green Bear...........300.00
Rosie................200.00
14" Pink Bear........300.00
15" Pink Bear........400.00
Page 132 & 133
Undressed 24" Bear...300.00
Dressed 24" Bear.....450.00
17" Gold Mohair......350.00
17" Gold Tin Eyes....325.00
12" Teddy............275.00
Page 134 & 135
13" Gold Mohair......250.00
15" Cotton Plush.....200.00
Pince Nez Bear.......195.00
Roosevelt Pin.........35.00
Bear Cart.............85.00
19" Cotton Bear......225.00
Older Golliwog........95.00
12" Brown Bear.......200.00
Helene...............325.00
Page 136 & 137
10" Brown Bear........75.00
14" Orange Bear.......85.00
8" Panda..............95.00
Waif.................400.00
Page 138 & 139
English Panda........325.00
18" Panda............425.00
Steiff from 1950's...450.00
Page 140 & 141
23" Cinnamon Bear....400.00
15" White Mohair.....300.00
Book.................150.00
23" Cinnamon Bear....250.00
20" Cinnamon Mohair..300.00
Page 142 & 143
Brown Mohair Bear....575.00
English Teddy........550.00
12" Gold Mohair......250.00
Dog..................200.00
16" Mohair...........275.00
Page 144 & 145
16" Gold Mohair......250.00
12" Gold Mohair......175.00
Fred & Minnie....pr. 500.00
Kiss Blowing Bear....275.00
20" Caramel Mohair...300.00
Page 146 & 147
28" Cotton Plush Bear..425.00
Grandpa Bear.........275.00
17" White Mohair.....250.00
Print.................35.00
Page 148 & 149
14" Gold Mohair......300.00
13" White Mohair.....200.00
17" Teddy............300.00
12" Bear.............275.00
15" White Wool Bear..200.00
Page 150 & 151
Farmer Bear..........250.00
Steiff Lamb..........150.00
16" Cinnamon Bear....250.00
17" Yellow Mohair....300.00
Dog...................95.00
17" White Mohair.....300.00
Page 152 & 153
13½" Brown Bear......200.00

14" Shaggy Bear......250.00
19" Gold Mohair......300.00
Cart.................100.00
16" Cinnamon Bear....250.00
Cat..................175.00
15" Yellow Mohair....225.00
11" Brown Mohair.....185.00
13" Brown Bear.......225.00
Page 154 & 155
Red Riding Hood......150.00
11" Brown Plush Bear...95.00
22" Yellow Mohair....325.00
24" Gold Mohair......350.00
Steiff Puppy..........50.00
Cocker Spaniel........50.00
Page 156 & 157
14" Teddy.............45.00
21" Pink Bear........250.00
17" White Cotton Plush.150.00
Book..................50.00
10" Dachshund.........85.00
9" Yellow Mohair.....135.00
Page 158 & 159
9" Beige Bear.........75.00
10" Sandy............125.00
Cloth Doll............50.00
16" Bear.............125.00
18" White Wool Bear..150.00
13" Sheepskin Bear....80.00
9" Pink Bear..........25.00
12½" Younger Bear.....75.00
Wicker Set............40.00
Page 160 & 161
13" Grey Mohair......225.00
Bruin Pull Toy.......175.00
Pull Toy Bear..900.00-1,200.00
Page 162 & 163
Riding Bear....900.00-1,200.00
13" Bear on Wheels...650.00
Steiff Pull Toy......700.00
Gulliver.............500.00
Page 164 & 165
Riding Bear/Pull Toy...600.00
10" Bear..............85.00
Bear on Wheels.......500.00
12" Gold Mohair......475.00
Hankie................10.00
Page 166
Pull Toy.............185.00
9" Teddy Bear........165.00
Page 168 & 169
6' Bear............1,700.00
1941 Steiff Bear.....400.00
19" Steiff...........600.00
Chad Valley..........700.00
32" Brown Bear.......200.00
34" Gold Bear........250.00
29" Gold Bear........250.00
13" Brown/Gold Bear...95.00
13" Golden Mohair....200.00
Page 170 & 171
15" Gund.............200.00
Andy Panda............95.00
Book..................15.00
18" Black Bear........75.00
17" Cinnamon Mohair..135.00
Scotch Bearkin.......250.00
6" Steiff............175.00
8" Steiff............225.00
3½" Steiff...........225.00
21" Spotted Bear.....195.00
Page 172 & 173
9" Beige Steiff......225.00
11" German Import....250.00
British Bear.........350.00
Cuddly Bear...........85.00
21" Schuco Teddy...1,150.00
13" Schuco Teddy.....700.00

Page 174 & 175
22" Schuco.........1,200.00
11" Beige Bear.......295.00
14" Beige Bear.......375.00
9" German Import.....200.00
22" Cotton Plush Bear..55.00
8" Wooly Plush Bear...15.00
Picnic Bear..........200.00
Teddy Bear Pitcher....15.00
15" Standing Bear....300.00
Page 176 & 177
14" Character Bear....35.00
Bass..................20.00
18" Bassist..........225.00
Piano/stool...........55.00
Violin................15.00
25" Pianist..........275.00
Drum.................150.00
17½" Drummer.........185.00
10" Gold Mohair......225.00
13" Steiff...........450.00
Page 178 & 179
18" Ideal Smokey......45.00
18" No. 2 Smokey......75.00
16" Smokey............55.00
4¼" Smokey............10.00
Punkinheads......ea. 250.00
Bear on Wheels.......225.00
1955 Brown Mohair....275.00
Page 180 & 181
Black Bear...........150.00
Knickerbocker........175.00
19" Gund, 17" Plushea. 200.00
9" White Mohair......135.00
Reddish-brown Mohair.135.00
Cuddly Twins.....ea. 30.00
Page 182 & 183
11" Teddy Baby.......550.00
Shaggy Brown Mohair..225.00
9" Steiff.............75.00
11" Teddy Baby.......600.00
21" Grisly...........400.00
9" Steiff "Zotty,"...135.00
8" Steiff Panda......265.00
15" Steiff "Zotty,"..225.00
11" Steiff "Cosy Teddy"110.00
10" Hermann..........115.00
Steiff Panda Bear....265.00
9" Panda..............40.00
Page 184 & 185
12" Panda.............20.00
13" Steiff Panda.....450.00
12" Black & White Panda.65.00
9" Panda Radio........45.00
13" Plush Panda.......20.00
"Koala Bear".........135.00
"Zotty"..............150.00
German Giant.........350.00
14" Grey/Beige Wool Bear75.00
5" Japanese Mohair....25.00
Page 186 & 187
18" Bear..............90.00
6" Blond Mohair......175.00
11" Beige Mohair......45.00
18" Steiff...........185.00
11" "Floppy Zotty"....85.00
6½" "Floppy Zotty"....55.00
Hand Puppet...........65.00
Page 188 & 189
Dish..................65.00
Winnie The Pooh.......75.00
Polar Bear...........150.00
22" Wool Bear........250.00
Christmas Bear........25.00
Page 190 & 191
Child's Bear..........35.00
Ideal Bear...........35.00
"Gentle Ben".........55.00

Knickerbocker Bears..ea. 20.00
"Petsy"..............125.00
Page 192 & 193
26" Steiff...........300.00
12" "Cosy Teddy".....125.00
Hermann Cuddly Bear..115.00
7½" "Cosy Teddy"......75.00
Page 194 & 195
"Cosy Orsi"...........40.00
16" Wooden Bear.......20.00
13" Synthetic Plush...35.00
"Bashful".............35.00
13" White Bear........60.00
Peggy Nisbet Bear.....85.00
Page 196 & 197
Chan..................20.00
Elizabeth Bear-et Browning
..................65.00
Amelia Bear-heart.....95.00
Advertising Bearsea. 20.00-25.00
Page 198
Floppy Bear..........150.00
Page 200 & 201
42" Brown Bear.......425.00
Book, "Misha".........35.00
Misha Bears.....per inch 1.50
36" Hermann Bear.....900.00
Page 202 & 203
Papa Bear............550.00
Mama and Baby........350.00
Artist Bears...ea. 85.00-125.00
"Debonair Bear," 1st...500.00
Page 204 & 205
18" Grey Fur Bear....120.00
Bellhop Bear.........125.00
Brown Baby Boy.......100.00
20" Artist Bear......100.00
Running Rabbit........45.00
Sitting Rabbit........45.00
Page 206
Artist's Bear........200.00
"Shirley-o-Bear"......75.00
Bear Rug..............95.00
Page 208 & 209
European Mechanical.1,200.00
Perfume Bottles......ea. 15.00
Perfume Bottle Bear..375.00
Page 210 & 211
Santa Clara Bear......65.00
Teddy Bear Muff......250.00
Embroidery Work......350.00
Lithograph Blocks....200.00
Teddy Muff...........200.00
Child's Muff.........150.00
Page 212 & 213
Oil Panted Photograph..300.00
Portrait..............25.00
Child's service......250.00
Page 214 & 215
Dish..................35.00
Toboggan Teddies soap..95.00
Tomato Can............45.00
Postcards......ea. 10.00-15.00
Page 216
Inkwell...............95.00
Book..................65.00
Page 218 & 219
17" Monkey Man.....2,500.00
Yes/No Bellhop Monkey.275.00
Chimp, white..........55.00
"Coco"................55.00
Steiff Cat on Wheels...500.00
Ichabod............2,800.00
21½" German........2,800.00
Page 220 & 221
22" Ger. Character...2,800.00
Unwigged Doll......2,500.00
German Postal Carrier.2,500.00

Page 222 & 223
Inspection Sargeant...2,500.00
Steiff Girl............850.00
11″ Girl & Boy Pair...1,500.00
Steiff Bird.............55.00
Steiff Beauty.........750.00
Page 224 & 225
Leprechaun...........850.00
11″ Steiff Girl........800.00
Dog Pull Toy.........500.00
Tea Cosey...........850.00
16″ Steiff Doll........450.00
14″ Steiff Doll........750.00
Steiff "Lucki".........200.00
Squirrel Hand Puppet...25.00
Page 226
"Mecki" & "Micki".....35.00
Mecki Children......ea. 30.00
Panda................150.00
Page 228 & 229
Steiff Donkey.........700.00
Steiff Camel..........700.00
Steiff Dachshund......300.00
Elephant.............600.00
Monkey...............125.00
Pug Dog.............750.00
St. Bernard..........900.00
Page 230 & 231
King "Leo"...........750.00
Zebra................500.00
Donkey...............550.00
Buster Brown's Dog...300.00
"Bully" dog..........250.00
Page 232 & 233
7″ Mickey Mouse.....650.00
5¼″ Minnie Mouse....650.00
"Cockie".............45.00
4½″ Mohair "Bully"..ea. 95.00
Cottontail............135.00
Page 234 & 235
Colt.................125.00
Fox Terrier...........150.00
Polar Bears.......pr. 1,500.00
Page 236 & 237
"Susi"...............135.00
"Fluffy".............85.00
Steiff Dog...........150.00
Kitty................110.00
Page 238
Dog.................135.00
"Chow-Chow Brownie"..165.00
Page 240 & 241
Steiff Ark............650.00
Musical Cat..........300.00
Sitting Siamese.......150.00
"Mopsy".............75.00

"Lizzy"..............75.00
"Susi"..............55.00
Page 242 & 243
Mama "Kitty Cat".......85.00
Kittens..............45.00
6½″ "Kitty Cat".......85.00
4″ "Kitty Cat".......75.00
"Topsy".............45.00
"Snurry"............135.00
5½″ "Tabby".........75.00
4″ "Tabby".........45.00
3½″ "Tabby".........45.00
17″ Puss 'N Boots....200.00
Page 244 & 245
10″ Puss 'N Boots.....150.00
White Cat............25.00
Black Cat............75.00
"Cosy Siam".........55.00
Page 246 & 247
"Molly".............95.00
"Foxy".............75.00
"Floppy Beagle".....55.00
"Tessie"............125.00
Dalmatian...........250.00
Copies of Pets.......ea 50.00
Page 248 & 249
"Snobby"............35.00
"Zotty".............150.00
"Cockie"............95.00
"Floppy Cat & Cockie"..45.00
"Ginny's Pup".......150.00
4″ "Peky"..........35.00
6″ "Peky"..........50.00
Page 250 & 251
"Hexie".............40.00
Monkey..............95.00
"Waldi"............150.00
Rabbit..............65.00
"Record Hansi"......175.00
"Niki"..............175.00
Page 252 & 253
Rabbits............ea. 45.00
"Manni"............125.00
11″ "Begging Rabbit"..125.00
11½″ Puppet.........45.00
"Lamby"............75.00
Black Lamb..........85.00
6½″ "Cow"..........80.00
"Floppy Lamb".....45.00
Donkey..............175.00
9½″ Pull Toy Cow.....295.00
"Lamby"............55.00
Pink Felt Pig.........40.00
Page 254 & 255
"Lamby"............45.00
"Floppy Lamby".......135.00

"Baby Goat"..........65.00
"Guinea Pig"........25.00
"Porcupine"..........35.00
Goldfish.............165.00
Felix................65.00
"Pony".............45.00
"Chimpanzee", brown...45.00
"Chimpanzee", white....55.00
Pig.................55.00
Page 256 & 257
"Eric the Bat".......250.00
Lion Cub............15.00
Page 258 & 259
Spider...............225.00
"Crabby"............200.00
"Gaty".............150.00
Elephant Head........300.00
Page 260 & 261
"Kangoo"............250.00
"Moosy"............225.00
"Wild Boar".........135.00
Page 262 & 263
"Bison"............200.00
Dromedary Camel.....200.00
17″ Llama...........225.00
11″ Llama...........85.00
6½″ Llama..........65.00
Page 264 & 265
Fox.................450.00
13½″ Tiger..........85.00
28″ Tiger...........400.00
22″ Tiger...........125.00
25″ Tiger...........350.00
29″ Tiger...........350.00
7″ Tiger, Japan, 7″...15.00
9″ Steiff Tiger......55.00
6″ Steiff Tiger......45.00
Cubs & Rhino.......ea 45.00
Page 266 & 267
"Leo"..............350.00
"Lion Cub"..........85.00
Giraffe..............375.00
45″ King Lion "Leo"....600.00
16″ "Lion Cub".......175.00
19″ "Cub"...........400.00
Leopard.............125.00
5½″ "Lion Cub"......55.00
Page 268 & 269
5″ Lion Sitting.......45.00
11″ King Lion "Leo".....65.00
4½″ Lion Standing......45.00
"Lea"..............55.00
Ideal Lion...........15.00
3″ Elephant.........85.00
8½″ Elephant........95.00
"Cosy Trampy".......65.00

Page 270 & 271
17″ "Okapi".........225.00
6½″ "Okapi".......55.00
"Zebra"............85.00
Panther.............150.00
"Coco".............55.00
Page 272 & 273
"Jocko"............125.00
"Record Peter"......175.00
"Elephant".........35.00
"Bambi"............35.00
Plate...............25.00
Page 274 & 275
"Bocky"............65.00
"Perri"............45.00
"Possy"............45.00
"Xorry"............45.00
"Cosy Fuzzy".......55.00
"Cosy Zicky".......55.00
Page 276 & 277
"Mountain Lamb"....55.00
10″ "Nagy".........175.00
6½″ "Nagy".......85.00
4″ "Nagy".........45.00
"Raccy"............45.00
Porcupine...........55.00
"Joggi"............45.00
Page 278 & 279
"Murmy"............55.00
"Diggy"............55.00
14″ Seal............85.00
"Slo"..............35.00
Page 280 & 281
"Robby"............45.00
"Paddy"............55.00
"Slo"..............95.00
"Froggy"............35.00
"Pieps".............30.00
"Wittie"............35.00
Page 282 & 283
Penguin.............95.00
"Goose".............65.00
Duck................55.00
Page 284 & 285
"Cock" & ducks.....ea 20.00
Chickens............20.00
"Teddyli", "Bibbie", "Cocoli"
.................ea 150.00
Hide-A-Gift Bunnys....ea 75.00
Page 286 & 287
"Waldili"...........225.00
"Zipper Nauty".......125.00
"Jolly Cockie".......125.00
Page 288
Hand Puppets.........25.00
"Zebra"............45.00

Page 11
Bear House 500.00
6″ Billie Possum . . . . 375.00+
3½″ Early Steiff . . . . . . 450.00+
3½″ Bear (1930) 250.00
3½″ Steiff (1905) . . . . . 450.00+
Chest 20.00
Page 12
3½″ Steiff, worn 165.00
Bisque Jtd. . . ea. 325.00-400.00
All bisque . . . . set 75.00
6″ Bear 250.00
Dog 25.00
Page 13
5″ German 185.00
4″ Sparse Mohair 35.00
4¾″ Cotton Plush 45.00
Wagon 25.00
6″ Blue/grey 85.00
Book 45.00
8″ ''Yorkie'' 350.00
7″ Japan 35.00
8″ Schuco . . . . 450.00+
Truck 45.00
Page 14
Bears on sofa . . . . . . ea. 45.00
Keywind 55.00
3½″ White Steiff . . . . . 275.00+
3″ Clemens 55.00
2½″ Schuco 125.00
3½″ Steiff (1950s) 225.00
5″ Clemens 45.00
Page 15
Teddy Music Box 55.00
Berlin Bear 40.00
5½″ Prickly Mohair . . . ea. 55.00
Berg Animals . . . . . . ea. 35.00
Page 16
Teddy Bears' Picnic . . . 3,000.00
4½″ Wood Teddy 15.00
Drum . . . . C.S.P
5″ Souvenir Bears . . . . . ea. 5.00
Clown Bear 65.00
Clown Muff 50.00
Lady Bear 80.00
Angel Bear 35.00
Page 17
5 Steiff Bears . . . . N.P.A.
17″ Gutta-percha 1,400.00
Page 18
21″ Rod Bear . . . . 3,500.00+
23″ ''Kellie'' . 3,000.00-3,500.00+
Page 19
16″ ''Tyler'' . . . . 1,500.00+
10″ White Steiff . . . . . 1,000.00+
Page 20
16″ Blank Button . . . . 1,800.00+
16″ ''Pearlie'' 1,400.00
Page 21
14″ Steiff . . . . 1,400.00+
Washstand . . . . 550.00+
10″ Steiff 750.00
Doll 600.00
Page 22
12″ Steiff ''Otto'' 900.00
12″ Bears . . . . ea. 900.00
Roadster 1,200.00
9″ Bear, worn 450.00
Wind-up 55.00
Page 23
12″ Steiff 750.00
12½″ Ltd. Ed. (1983) . . 150.00
17″ Twins . . . . pr. 3,500.00
Stroller 125.00
Page 24
20″ ''Daddy's Bear'' . . . 325.00
11″ Steiff 275.00

22″ Bear . . . . 2,800.00+
13″ Polar Bear 700.00
Page 25
13½″ Steiff 900.00
12″ ''Eustace'' . . . . . 1,200.00+
16″ Steiff 1,100.00
Page 26
18″ ''Harry'' 1,100.00
19″ ''Aunt Maggie'' 400.00
8″ ''Mr. Steiff'' 550.00
11″ American . . . . 550.00+
Clown & Donkey . . . . ea. 115.00
Props . . . . ea. 10.00
16″ Velvet Nose 800.00
Page 27
13″ Topsy-Turvy . . . . 1,200.00+
14½″ Ideal 700.00
11½″ ''Allie'' . . . . 550.00+
12″ ''Fran'' 900.00
Page 28
13″ ''Arnold'' . . . . 650.00+
12″ ''Amanda'' 400.00
22″ Drummer Boy . . . . 1,000.00+
Drum 150.00
16″ Bear 350.00
Page 29
14″ Ideal 600.00
12″ Ideal 600.00
Photo Postcard 18.00
Page 30
19″ Unknown Maker . . . 800.00+
13″ Bruin Mfg. Co. 575.00
24″ Off-white . . . . . . 1,200.00+
Page 31
17″ Knobby Fabric 200.00
22″ Mohair Bear 1,000.00
18″ Black Velour 200.00
Stroller 75.00
Page 32
21″ Standing Bear 350.00
10″ Bear 600.00
Page 33
16″ ''Rosie'' 1,200.00
20″ ''Doc'' 900.00
9½″ Bear 300.00
Dolls . . . . ea. 275.00
Page 34
18″ Large Bruin 900.00
10″ Burlap-type 150.00
20″ Bear 450.00
27″ Bear 625.00
Page 35
Vintage Photo/bear 18.00
12″ Bear 425.00
Book 20.00
22″ Gold Bear 550.00
Doll 195.00
Page 36
19″ ''Boonie'' 500.00
16½″ ''Cricket'' 400.00
26″ Ideal Bear 650.00
Page 37
22″ American 475.00
Doll 500.00
Old spectacles 10.00
20″ Bear 500.00
Wagon . . . . 200.00+
18″ Musical 400.00
22″ Bear 575.00
Page 38
12½″ (if perfect) 125.00
11″ Bisque 300.00
22″ ''Nifty'' 650.00
19″ Bear 425.00
Books . . . . ea. 150.00
Page 39
30″ White Bear . . . . . . 900.00+
17″ ''Lord D'Arcy'' 350.00

Pencil Case 35.00
6″ On All Fours 200.00
Steiff Panda 175.00
Page 40
20″ American Bear 500.00
Dog 125.00
26″ Electric-eye Bear . . 600.00
Marx Wind-up 200.00
8″ Gold Mohair 135.00
Page 41
26″ Steiff (1922) . . . . 2,000.00+
12″ Bear 450.00
21½″ English 500.00
Page 42
20½″ Bears . . . . . . ea. 300.00
14″ ''Peter'' . . . . 1,800.00+
Med. Size Bristle . . . ea. 150.00
Page 43
14″ Bear/socks 150.00
Horse 500.00
12″ ''Murf'' 100.00
18″ Helvetic Bear . . . . 1,000.00+
Page 44
11½″ Patchwork 185.00
18″ ''Vernon'' (worn) . . . 75.00
24″ Gbr. Sussenguth . 1,000.00
Page 45
19″ Honey Bear 400.00
24″ Cotton Plush 285.00
Steiff Mole 35.00
22″ Marching Bear 450.00
Page 46
14″ Petsy (1928) . . . . 1,600.00+
18″ Clown (1928) . . . 1,200.00+
23″ Drum Major 450.00
Page 47
20½″ Clown Bear . . . . 1,500.00+
12″ Helvetic, worn 450.00
16″ German Bear . . . . . 500.00+
Page 48
9″ Bear 125.00
Keystone Train 250.00
18″ ''Poor Fred'' 350.00
10″ Frosted Mohair . . . 200.00
10″ ''Hot-cha'' 200.00
Page 49
Vintage Photo 15.00
16″ Mohair Bear 325.00
13″ Porridge Bear 275.00
Page 50
20″ ''Bearly Pink'' 325.00
Horse 600.00
14″ Musical (1930s) . . . 250.00
Horse 500.00
19½″ ''Tasi'' 350.00
Page 51
13″ Sledding Bear 225.00
8½″ ''Renny'' 125.00
7″ Son 125.00
14″ Father 200.00
13″ Tin Decal Eyes . . . 275.00
Page 52
23″ Grey Mohair 375.00
9″ Boy (''Cheeky'') 15.00
9″ Girl (worn) 70.00
13½″ Steiff Bear 900.00
Page 53
36″ ''Rosamond'' . . . . 1,000.00+
17″ Bear/book 350.00
17″ Lady Bear 300.00
Print 15.00
Page 54
29″ Cotton Plush 350.00
26″ Chad Valley 700.00
19″ Steiff 600.00
14″ Sleep Eye 150.00
Page 55
21″ Mohair Bear 700.00

17″ Rabbit 150.00
12″ Tin Nose 200.00
11″ Bear 65.00
Duck 35.00
Page 56
6″ ''Teddy Baby'' . . . . . 600.00+
9″ Panda 85.00
8″ Rayon Velour 65.00
18″ ''Francesca'' 100.00
Page 57
21″ Steiff Bear 900.00
12″ Cotton Plush 800.00
16½″ White Mohair . . . 175.00
Page 58
8½″ Bear 225.00
6″ Bear 175.00
Valentine 15.00
10″ Bear Boy 50.00
25″ Vinyl Face 45.00
Page 59
28″ Brown Bear 450.00
14″ Hermann KG Bear . . 250.00
28″ ''Great Bear'' 425.00
24″ Knickerbocker 300.00
9″ Clemens 65.00
Page 60
20″ ''Jennifer'' 200.00
20″ Character 185.00
12½″ Twyford 125.00
Page 61
Shaggy Gold Bear 250.00
20″ Character 250.00
5″ Cub 40.00
15½″ Twyford (1930s) . . 225.00
20″ Twyford (1950s) . . . 175.00
Page 62
11″ Mohair Bear 350.00
17″ English 250.00
14″ Swiss Musical 175.00
2½″ Mini Schuco 100.00
Page 63
''Orig. Teddy,'' 3½″ 200.00-225.00
6″ 175.00
7″ 200.00
8½″ 225.00
10″ 250.00-275.00
13½″ 300.00-325.00
16″ 350.00-400.00
14″ Smokey (complete) . . 150.00
Page 64
13″ Steiff Bear 325.00
6″ Steiff Bear 175.00
Wheeled Toy 20.00
20″ Steiff Bear 600.00
Book 7.00
Page 65
13″ Steiff 325.00
17″ Cat 30.00
14″ Sleep Eyes 25.00
15″ Pouting Bear 25.00
Page 66
13½″ Music Bear . . . . . 650.00+
8½″ White Bear 75.00
Steiff Giraffe 75.00
Ideal Bear 400.00
Page 67
Koala Bears . . . . ea. 15.00-20.00
10½″ Steiff 250.00
8½″ Steiff Koala . . . . . 350.00+
5″ Steiff Koala . . . . 135.00+
Page 68
5″ Polar Bear 95.00
6½″ Polar Bear 125.00
10″ Polar Bear 275.00
8½″ ''Teddy Baby'' 400.00
19½″ ''Jocko'' 200.00
Page 69
12″ American Panda . . . 100.00

12" Ideal Bear.........75.00
17" Hermann KG.....275.00
"Cosy Blanko".........35.00
Page 70
9" Kamar.............65.00
6" Dog...............5.00
18" Panda............150.00
6" Steiff Panda......200.00+
8½" Steiff Panda.....275.00+
Page 71
11" White "Zotty".....275.00+
Steiff Postcard........12.00
6½" "Zotty"..........135.00
8½" "Zotty"..........135.00
12½" "Zotty".........165.00
18" "Zotty"..........250.00
Book................25.00
Page 72
21" Grisly...........85.00
29" Grisly...........125.00
11" "Zooby"..........375.00
8" Clemens..........95.00
Page 73
22" Character........35.00
15" Knickerbocker....25.00
8" Bear/Wagon.......200.00+
Page 74
7" White Berg........100.00
5¾" Gold Berg........50.00
12½" Walkman........45.00
11" hermann Zotty....135.00
Stocking.............45.00
Page 75
5" Hermann KG.......75.00
Page 76
7½" "Cosy Teddy".....75.00
8½" "Lully Baby".....55.00
8" "Cosy Orsi".......40.00
10" Elvis Bear.......75.00
11" "Minky Zotty"....175.00
Page 77
9" Animal Fair.......ea. 6.00
14" Eden Toys........18.00
16" "Banker Bear"....18.00
Page 78
25" Lambskin.........100.00
16" "Teddy Bear".....75.00
Page 79
12" Misha............35.00
Teddy Bear Tea Party..300.00
Page 80
16" "Klein Archie"....150.00
11" "Seebar".........50.00
Page 81
15" "Edwardian"......85.00
16" "Long Snout".....125.00
11½" Panda (1984)....100.00
13½" Panda (1984)....135.00
9" Red Grisly........30.00
Page 82
63" Polar Bear.......1,200.00
16" Bremen Bear......60.00
1984 Goldilocks Set...350.00
Page 83
Artist Bears....250.00-1,000.00
36" "Easter Bunny"...800.00
Page 84
18" "Mr. Cinnamon"...300.00
16" "Angel Moran"....85.00
8" Mink Bear.........125.00
Page 85
33" "Fritz"..........500.00
18½" "Klein Fritz"...200.00
23" "Boscoe".........250.00
Page 86
"Spike".........45.00 & 88.00
14" "Yodee"..........50.00
15" "Rough Rider"....150.00

14" "Liberty Bear".....135.00
Page 87
17" Artist Bear.........75.00
10" Steiff.............75.00
22" "Ouchy".........75.00
24" King.............175.00
12" T.R..............65.00
8" Hermann KG.......38.00
Shirt................3.00
Page 88
8½" Bruin...........700.00+
30" Bear............3,000.00+
Page 89
17" Steiff...........1,700.00+
11" Elephant........700.00
13" Goat............700.00
Page 90
15" Teddy Bear.......250.00
13½" Bear/Wheels....900.00
10" "Record Teddy"...550.00+
7" Bear.............125.00
Page 91
25" Hand Wagon.....100.00
19½" "Jocko" (1975)...85.00
23" Horse............300.00
19" Shaggy Monkey....75.00
11" Rushton Monkey....45.00
13" Rayon Velour.....275.00
Page 92
11" Terrier..........75.00
9½" Steer...........350.00
10" Cat.............250.00
10" Dog.............200.00
Page 93
20" Tiger............550.00
23" Bear............300.00
19" Steiff (if mint)....500.00
31½" Pony...........600.00
Page 94
8" Rabbit............395.00
6" Possum...........250.00+
9" Polar Bear........1,600.00+
Page 95
13" Tumbler.........900.00+
8" Schuco Bear......375.00+
24" Store Display....550.00
Page 96
6½" Keywind Dog.....45.00
11" Irish Terrier.....100.00
13" Tumbler.........150.00
7" Terrier...........50.00
9½" Drinking Bear....75.00
Page 97 & 98.......N.P.A.
Page 99
3½" Compact Bear....400.00
4½" Bear (1950).......75.00
4½" Perfume Bear....375.00
3¼" Pink Bear.......400.00
Kilgore Highchair....25.00
3½" Green Monkey....400.00
2½" Early Bear......250.00
Page 100
7" Penguin..........375.00+
10" Walking Bear.....900.00+
7" Yes/No Cat.......425.00
Page 101
5" Yes/No Specs......425.00
5" Yes/No Bear.......425.00
13" Bear............650.00+
15" Redressed Bear...450.00
Page 102
12" Lift Boy.........275.00
Yes/No Monkey......N.P.A.
14" Bear............750.00+
Page 103
10" Bear............425.00
3" Jumping Frog......75.00
6" Keywind..........95.00

13" "Tricky".........600.00
Miniatures.........ea. 100.00
Page 104
Lonely Doll Books....ea. 20.00
8" "Tricky" Cat......375.00
20" Yes/No.........1,000.00
Page 105
14" Cat.............75.00
14" Goofy...........45.00
4½" Keywind........125.00
Page 106
Books.............ea. 25.00
3½" Mickey/Minnie.ea. 150.00
Page 107
3" Mutt.............110.00
2½" Puppy..........110.00
3½" Soccer Bear....125.00+
Miniatures.........ea. 100.00
Panda..............150.00
Tumbling Bear.......100.00
Tumbling (working)...400.00
Page 108
10" Billie Possum....450.00+
Postcard............20.00
Button.............20.00
Spoon..............45.00
Old Print...........45.00
Book...............95.00+
Page 109
8½" Paper Doll.......35.00
11½" Raphael Tuck...65.00+
Spoon/Fork MIB.....50.00
8" Candy Container...350.00
Page 110
10" Muff (1910).......300.00
13" "Cheeky" Muff....150.00
7" Kitty Muff........125.00
Page 111
8½" Ideal Muff.......225.00
14" Pj. Bag Teddy....250.00
6¾" Figurine........95.00
Page 112
7" Paper Teddy.......35.00
Bear Brand Box......15.00
Puzzle.............20.00
20" Bear............300.00
Valentines........ea. 5.00-10.00
6" Bank.............65.00
Tape Measure.......35.00
Buttons.........ea. 15.00+
Page 113
Goldilocks Print.....45.00
Sign...............25.00
Bottle..............15.00
Salt Shaker.........10.00
Friction Toy.........35.00
Page 114
Pattern Book.........10.00
18½" Golliwog.....ea. 55.00+
11" Merrythought....45.00+
16" Golliwog........55.00+
15" Artist Golliwog...25.00
8" Bear.............15.00
Page 115
12½" Golliwog.......45.00+
China Set...........250.00+
Valentine...........15.00
12½" Golliwog.......45.00+
15" Bear............200.00
Golliwog Mugs......ea. 5.00
Page 116
Peter Bull..........C.S.P.
2½" Schuco Cat......110.00
Jenny Lind/Cat......475.00
Wooden Bear........15.00
20" Lion............350.00
8½" Lamb...........75.00
Bisque Doll.........1,200.00

Page 117
24" Feco Boxer.......75.00
24" Feco Spaniel.....70.00
20" Lenci Doll.......525.00
Book...............4.00
Bear...............15.00
Barbie MIB.........15.00
Page 118
Lori 'N Rori.........175.00+
Cristina's Bear......35.00+
Michael/Bear........450.00
Page 119
15" Papa............65.00
12" Mama...........70.00
8" Baby............38.00
Goldilocks/Taffeta...125.00
Page 120
12" Dumbo..........65.00
19" Krazy Kat.......650.00+
12" Ferdinand.......150.00
Book...............25.00
Page 121
16" Bugs Bunny......95.00
3½" Dog............45.00
15" Tiger...........55.00
Book...............20.00
Page 122
13" Pooh...........95.00
13" Bonzo..........350.00+
9" Daisy...........135.00
Page 123
8" Vinyl Snoopy.....30.00
Homemade Pooh.....15.00
Homemade Eeyore...15.00
Paddington/Lucy....pr. 250.00
Page 124
16" Baloo..........200.00+
10" King Louie......85.00
8" Baby Hathi.......85.00
10" Bagheera.......150.00+
13½" Shere Khan....125.00
Page 125
Wacky Mackys.......ea. 15.00
12" Bear............35.00
7½" Doll............85.00
Book...............20.00
Page 126
16" Super Ted.......75.00
13½" Green Man....95.00+
Page 127
1st Kellogs Set......250.00
Lora...............35.00
Hansel.............15.00
"Gaty".............25.00
Teddy Baby.........65.00
Older Steiff.........125.00
Felpa..............75.00
Page 128
Hide-a-Gift........ea. 75.00
2½"..............ea. 20.00
MIB...............100.00
5" Kisses...........6.00
"Tuffy"............30.00
Page 129
19½" Jolly Fox......125.00
4½" Rabbit.........60.00
14" "Cupcake".......30.00
16" Crocker Bank....30.00
Page 130
16" "Big Pink".......25.00
13½" "Goldi".......95.00
Page 131
10" Rolly Clown.....1,800.00
Humpty Dumpty.....1,200.00
Page 132
17" Witch..........2,800.00
Gendarme...1,200.00-1,500.00

Page 133
14″ Lizzie............850.00
4″ Mohair Boar........45.00
Struwelpeter.........2,500.00
Page 134
14″ Olaf.............850.00
22″ Moor.............2,800.00
Page 135
15″ Fireman..........275.00
16″ Doll (1930s)......350.00
12½″ Santa...........350.00
7″ Santa.............250.00
12″ Puppet...........85.00
Page 136
Max/Moritz....pr. 250.00
7½″ "Clownie".........65.00
11″ "Cappy"..........65.00
Page 137
Caricatures......ea. 3,000.00
Page 138
Mech.....ea. 3,000.00-4,500.00
Page 139
20″ Horse.....ea. 1,500.00
17″ "Bully"..........2,000.00
Page 140
Dressed Ducks....ea. 900.00
Bandleader..........2,000.00
20″ Mech Bear......3,000.00
10″ Mech. Fox.....1,500.00
Page 141
Mech. Rooster......1,500.00
Rooster & Hen....ea. 1,100.00
"Bully"...ea. 1,500.00-2,000.00
13″ Trainer..........900.00
Page 142
Mech. Dogs....ea. 1,500.00
Mech. Elephants..ea. 2,000.00
13″ Pigs.....ea. 1,000.00
10″ Teddy Bear.....1,300.00 +
Page 143
Mech. Rabbit........1,200.00
Non-mech. Rabbits..ea. 900.00
Mech. Monkeys....ea 1,000.00
Non-mech. (worn).....200.00
Page 144
7½″ Ted.............95.00
9″ Foxes.........pr. 650.00
Page 145
Nimrod Set (1983......175.00
8½″ Hunter (1953)....400.00
9″ Rabbits.........pr. 550.00
Page 146
17″ Gund.............95.00
13½″ "Nikili".........275.00
13″ Yes/No Monkey....200.00
18″ Gund.............95.00
18″ Merrythought......100.00
Page 147
Mule & Goat.......ea. 30.00
30″ Doll............250.00
12″ "Ossili"..........125.00
House & Mouse.....set 75.00
3¼″ Grey Mouse......35.00
3¼″ White Mouse......30.00
Page 148
3½″ Dressed Mouse....50.00
Baby Bear............150.00
Dressed Bears......ea. 150.00
Panda...............150.00
Mini Schuco.....100.00-125.00
17″ "Rico" Rabbit....165.00
Page 149
10″ "Fluffy"..........250.00
14″ Pig..............300.00

11½″ Puss 'N Boots....300.00
Page 150
23½″ Monkey.........175.00
11½″ Bear...........900.00
13″ Poodle..........125.00
12″ Terrier...........65.00
15″ Spaniel..........200.00
Page 151
7″ Rabbit..........150.00
8½″ Yes/No..........375.00
8″ "Honey Boy"........450.00
Page 152
6″ Airdale..........165.00
2½″ Pom-Pom Bird....50.00
Page 153
10″ "Bully"..........300.00
5″ "Mopsy"..........35.00
13½″ Kangaroo........275.00
5½″ Skye Terrier.....225.00
Page 154
8½″ Grisly Dog........55.00
11½″ Dog (1930s)......70.00
10½″ Pony...........450.00
10″ Zebra...........70.00
Page 155
5½″ Rabbit..........150.00
9½″ Jointed Cat......200.00
Page 156
12″ Kersa..........125.00
16″ Gund...........40.00
4½″ Composition......55.00
4″ Red Bear.........20.00
5½″ Rattle Head.......40.00
Page 157
8½″ "Lizzy".........55.00
9″ "Cattie".........55.00
10″ "Fiffy".........135.00
Page 158
11″ Grisly..........65.00
4½″ Hermann KG......45.00
Page 159
4½″ Kitties....ea. 20.00-35.00
5½″ Tom Cat.........45.00
6½″ Boxer..........75.00
5″ "Snurry"........135.00 +
3½″ "Gussy".........65.00
4″ "Kitty-Cat".......85.00 +
Page 160
13″ Knickerbocker....65.00
5½″ Velvet Dog.......15.00
5½″ Scotty.........95.00
Page 161
21″ Merrythought.....125.00
13″ Sheep Dog........150.00
6½″ "Laika".........200.00 +
11″ "Otto"..........20.00
Page 162
6½″ "Beppo"........100.00
8½″ White Scotty....200.00 +
4″ White Chow.......125.00 +
Page 163
4″ "Bazi"...........50.00
4″ "Cockie".........65.00
6½″ "Cockie".........95.00
7″ "Collie".........110.00
Page 164
11″ "Revue Susi".......95.00
7½″ B&W "Cockie".....95.00
7″ Terrier...........25.00
4″ Spaniel..........15.00
6½″ Dalmatian.......50.00
Page 165
13½″ "Corso"........175.00
8½″ "Corso" (not shown)125.00

7″ Farnell Dog........45.00
10″ Dog.............65.00
13″ Nodder.............45.00
Page 166
7″ St. Bernard.......200.00 +
5″ R.C.A. Dog.......175.00 +
Page 167
11″ Foxterrier.......110.00
4″ Beagle..........50.00
9″ Hermann KG Poodle..45.00
Page 168
13″ "Waldi"..........55.00
11″ Dachshund........30.00
Page 169
3″ Pigs.........ea. 40.00
22″ Dakin...........C.S.P.
Barnyard Animals......C.S.P.
Page 170
13″ Bunny..........65.00
20″ Begging Rabbit....250.00
11½″ "Niki".........150.00
10″ Standing Rabbit...135.00
Page 171
10″ "Pummy"........95.00
6½″ "Vario".........75.00
5½″ "Lamby".........135.00
8½″ "Lamby".........150.00
4″ "Swapl"..........85.00
5½″ "Swapl".........125.00
10″ "Swapl".........250.00
13″ "Swapl".........300.00
Page 172
12″ Dinosaurs.....ea. 400.00 +
17″-29″ Dinos.....ea. 550.00 +
4″ Brown Squirrel....55.00
4″ Grey Squirrel....45.00
Page 173
16″ Bumble Bee.......35.00
4″ Skunk..........125.00 +
4″ Hippo..........45.00
Page 174
5½″ Bengal Tiger.....125.00
4″ Jointed Tiger Cub....95.00
8½″ Jointed Lion......85.00
Page 175
10″ Lynx..........175.00 +
Zebra............150.00
6″ Trophy Head.......35.00
5½″ Reclining.........60.00
5½″ Standing.........45.00
Page 176
13½″ "Loopy" Wolf....350.00 +
4½″ Panda..........75.00 +
6″ "Diggy".........60.00
12″ "Diggy".........175.00
9″ Steer..........200.00 +
8½″ "Yuku".........150.00 +
12″ "Yuku" (not shown).185.00
Page 177
36″ Tiger...........600.00 +
15½″ "Sulac".........300.00
15½″ "Zolac".........300.00
15½″ "Lulac".........150.00
7″ "Wiggy" & "Waggy".....
ea. 125.00
11″ Red Fox.........250.00
Page 178
4″ Snail...........125.00 +
11″ Mohair Frog......175.00
3½″-4″ Velvet Frogs.ea. 55.00
4″ Felt "Crabby".......125.00
7″ Felt "Crabby".......165.00 +
Page 179
4″ Lesser Panda......200.00 +

8″ Lesser Panda......350.00 +
10″ Giraffe..........65.00
6½″ "Xorry"..........95.00
Page 180
8½″ Petz Monkey......50.00
4″ Green Monkey......75.00
10″ "Mungo"........65.00
Page 181
12″ Orangutan........75.00
22″ Elephant.........450.00
8″ "Dormy".........85.00
8″ "Cosy Raggy".......55.00
Page 182
6″ Prairie Dog.......55.00
10″ Fawn...........65.00
6½″ "Trampy".........30.00
Page 183
Alpine Goats...ea. 45.00-65.00
Mtn. Rams....ea. 45.00-65.00
Giraffe.....1,800.00-2,300.00
Page 184
4″ Penguin..........55.00
Book...............5.00
8½″ "Peggy".........60.00
6½″ Pelican.........165.00 +
6½″ Stork..........165.00 +
Page 185
4″ Hen............55.00
6″ Floppy Hen.......95.00
11½″ Rooster.........95.00
5″ "Hucky"..........45.00
5″ Cosy Chick.......30.00
Page 186
4″ Duck............35.00
6½″ Goose.........75.00 +
8″ Colored Duck......75.00
5″ Finch...........50.00
2½″ Colored Duck.....25.00
1½″ Early Birds.....ea. 20.00
3½″ Raven..........25.00
2½″ Yellow Duck......25.00
2½″ Rabbits.......ea. 15.00
2″ Ladybug..........10.00
3″ Seagull..........25.00
Page 187
10″ Pigeon.........60.00
11½″ Owl...........C.S.P.
4¼″ Stork..........15.00
2″ Goose..........25.00
Page 188
8½″ Parrot.........85.00
19″ Cloth Doll......500.00
12″ Drake..........95.00
10½″ Swan..........75.00
Page 189
30″ Red Pheasant.....300.00
4″ "Tucky" Turkey....125.00
10″ Sailor Duck......75.00
Page 190
11″ Woodpecker.......150.00
5¼″ Parakeet.........35.00
5½″ "Putty" Turkey...95.00 +

On the Cover
20″ Steiff Teddy Bear...600.00
Title Page
8″ & 12″ Dinosaurs..ea 400.00
Back Cover
17″ "Dumpy Po....2,000.00 +

C.S.P. - Current Selling Price
N.P.A. - No Price Available

197

Schroeder's Antiques Price Guide

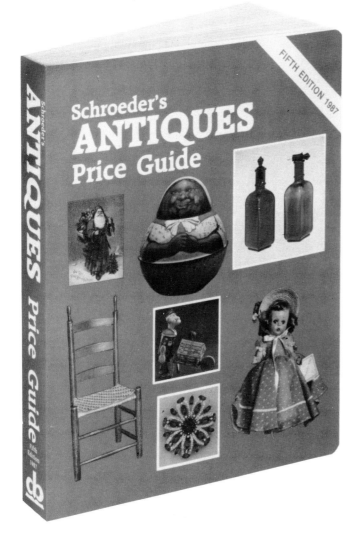

Schroeder's Antiques Price Guide has climbed its way to the top in a field already supplied with several well-established publications! The word is out, *Schroeder's Price Guide* is the best buy at any price. Over 500 categories are covered, with more than 50,000 listings. But it's not volume alone that makes Schroeder's the unique guide it is recognized to be. From ABC Plates to Zsolnay, if it merits the interest of today's collector, you'll find it in Schroeder's. Each subject is represented with histories and background information. In addition, hundreds of sharp original photos are used each year to illustrate not only the rare and the unusual, but the everyday "fun-type" collectibles as well -- not postage stamp pictures, but large close-up shots that show important details clearly.

Each edition is completely re-typeset from all new sources. We have not and will not simply change prices in each new edition. All new copy and all new illustrations make Schroeder's THE price guide on antiques and collectibles.

The writing and researching team behind this giant is proportionately large. It is backed by a staff of more than seventy of Collector Books' finest authors, as well as a board of advisors made up of well-known antique authorities and the country's top dealers, all specialists in their fields. Accurancy is their primary aim. Prices are gathered over the entire year previous to publication, from ads and personal contacts. Then each category is thoroughly checked to spot inconsistencies, listings that may not be entirely reflective of actual market dealings, and lines too vague to be of merit. Only the best of the lot remains for publication. You'll find *Schroeder's Antiques Price Guide* the one to buy for factual information and quality.

No dealer, collector or investor can afford not to own this book. It is available from your favorite bookseller or antiques dealer at the low price of $11.95. If you are unable to find this price guide in your area, it's available from Collector Books, P. O. Box 3009, Paducah, KY 42001 at $11.95 plus $1.00 for postage and handling.

8½ x 11, 608 Pages $11.95

COLLECTOR BOOKS
A Division of Schroeder Publishing Co., Inc.